Communicating the User Experience

Communicating the User Experience

A PRACTICAL GUIDE FOR CREATING USEFUL UX DOCUMENTATION

Richard Caddick
Steve Cable

A John Wiley and Sons, Ltd, Publication

This edition first published 2011

© 2011 Richard Caddick and Steve Cable

Registered office

John Wiley & Sons Ltd, The Atrium, Southern Gate, Chichester, West Sussex, PO19 8SQ, United Kingdom

For details of our global editorial offices, for customer services and for information about how to apply for permission to reuse the copyright material in this book, please see our Web site at www.wiley.com.

The right of the author to be identified as the author of this work has been asserted in accordance with the Copyright, Designs and Patents Act 1988.

Photography © James Chudley

978-1-119-97110-8

A catalogue record for this book is available from the British Library.

Set in 10/14 Chaparral Pro Light by Wiley Composition Services

Printed in the U.S. by Krehbiel

About the Authors

RICHARD CADDICK set up cxpartners, a user-centered design agency, with Giles Colborne in 2004 with the aim of creating measurable differences for clients they love to work with. Richard has worked as a consultant for several well-known global brands, including Expedia, Jaguar, HSBC, and Nokia. Richard's most at home in workshops surrounded by pens, paper and whiteboards trying to refine and improve designs for users.

STEVE CABLE, a user experience consultant for cxpartners, spends every day wireframing, testing, and crafting documents that communicate the needs of users. He's consulted for global hotel chains, car manufacturers, eCommerce websites, music management applications, mobile sites, and too many more to mention. As an illustrator and a lover of infographics, Steve feels it's important to produce documents that not only communicate clearly but are as visually interesting as the data that sits behind them.

Richard Caddick (left) and Steve Cable deliver user experience solutions for cxpartners.

Credits

Some of the people who helped bring this book to market include the following:

Editorial and Production

VP Consumer and Technology Publishing Director: Michelle Leete

Associate Director, Book Content Management: Martin Tribe

Associate Publisher: Chris Webb

Assistant Editor: Ellie Scott

Senior Project Editor: Sara Shlaer

Editorial Manager: Jodi Jensen

Editorial Assistant: Leslie Saxman

Development Editor: Box Twelve Communications, Inc.

Project Editor: Box Twelve Communications, Inc.

Technical Editor: Anthony Mace

Copy Editor: Maryann Steinhart

Photography: James Chudley

Marketing

Associate Marketing Director: Louise Breinholt

Marketing Executive: Kate Parrett

Composition Services

Compositor: Wiley Composition Services

Proof Reader: Susan Hobbs

Indexer: Potomac Indexing, LLC

For Katharine, Emilia, and Elise

—Richard Caddick

For Hannah and Freddie

—Steve Cable

Authors' Acknowledgments

This book couldn't have been written without the support of our colleagues at cxpartners: Jesmond Allen, Chris Berridge, Walt Buchan, James Chudley, Giles Colborne, Chloe Holbrook, Nik Lazell, Joe Leech, Rob Matthews, Amy McGuinness, James Rosenberg, Neil Schwarz, Jay Spanton, Chui Chui Tan, Anna Thompson, Verity Whitmore, and Fiz Yazdi. You've all helped to shape and transform the contents of this book.

We are hugely grateful to the support we've received from Wiley. In particular, Chris Webb for spotting the opportunity and chasing us down, Sara Shlaer for pointing us in the right direction, Jeff Riley for his unflappable patience with a couple of amateurs, and Jennifer Mayberry for her design talents.

Thanks to James Chudley: the photos you've taken make the book special and unique. We love them!

Anthony Mace, thank you for taking the time to make sure the text is clear and useful to practitioners.

Piers Alder and Jennie Blythe: thank you for reading through drafts and making improvements.

We are hugely grateful to our clients. Over the past seven years you have trusted us with your products and allowed us to collaborate with you in understanding your users and your business.

A personal thanks from Richard: Katharine, you will always be the best thing ever to happen to me. Emilia and Elise, you make every day brilliant. I love you all so much. Mum and Dad, you never pressured me into being someone that I wasn't, but you inspired and encouraged me to be who I am. Thank you.

A personal thanks from Steve: Hannah, thank you for supporting me through this and everything else in my life. You are amazing. Freddie, thank you for being the happiest, most fun (and craziest) son ever.

Contents

CHAPTER 5

Introduction

THE ROLE OF a user experience consultant, and specifically the user-centered design process, is to help guide and shape the development of products and services based on what the user understands and requires. To do this, the consultant needs to be a facilitator and communicator, ensuring that the right user information is uncovered and conveyed to the project stakeholders.

The purpose of the book is to help you communicate the user experience more effectively by producing insightful documents that successfully communicate the needs of the user to the business. It shows you what needs to go into the documents; what research needs to be done; ideas for facilitating practical workshops. These workshops are designed for the project team and stakeholders to help them understand user goals and behavior, enabling the team to collaborate on process, content and design solutions. This book also shows you how to work with PowerPoint, OmniGraffle, Axure, Word, or Excel to produce these documents (though the theory can be applied to many more applications beyond these, such as HTML prototyping).

The ultimate goal is for you to create better products and services that have a transformational, measurable, and lasting impact to their users.

We're mindful of the real-world constraints of time, budget, and resource availability, so throughout the book we've included straightforward ways to conduct research and produce documents (call center listening and rapid sketching can transform decision-making in minutes and hours rather than days and weeks). The fidelity of the output is less important than the message—although conversely, well-presented documents are often better received because they show care and rigor.

Each chapter is focused on key user experience documents and breaks down into:

> The purpose of the documentation.

> The information and emotional needs you are communicating.

> The project team you are communicating to.

> Ideas for research and workshops.

> The simplest and most effective ways to rapidly share outputs and ideas.

> Step-by-step instruction for how to develop documentation using common software programs (such as PowerPoint, OmniGraffle, Axure, and Excel).

We've spent thousands of hours running workshops, sketching ideas, and creating documents across hundreds of projects. We want to share the knowledge that we've found to be important so that you can improve what you are doing now (or get a head start in your career), and hope that in turn you help influence what we do in the future.

A summary of the documents

Figures 1 through 8 show each document and the specific user experience insights they provide for the project team.

FIGURE 1: Personas. Focusing the team on the users and their needs.

Goal: To find the perfect romantic city break

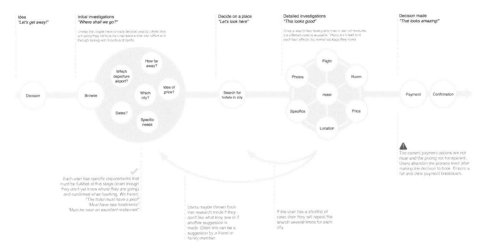

FIGURE 2: Task Models. Understanding user behavior.

Goal: To buy the items in my basket

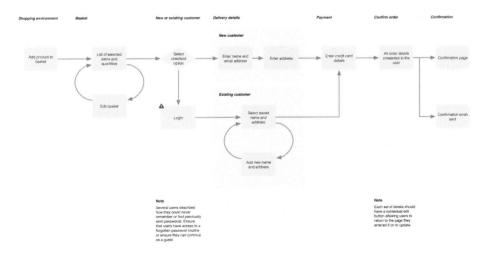

FIGURE 3: User Journeys. Showing how the system needs to match the user behavior.

Content requirements for choosing a boutique dress

How do users want content presented:

Photos – Large high quality photographs showing the front, back, detailing and a model shot. Copy – Clear and non-patronising. Users want to be reassured by the detailing, heritage and ethics.

Summary of core needs:

Pictures – What do the products look like? Price –Price, any applicable offers and easily accessibly delivery charges. Sizing and availability – What sizes are available and what are the dimensions of our sizing? Do they have my size? Delivery time – When will I get it?

ID	Page name	What must users do? The core purpose of the page.	What support do they need? Include quotes from research.	Required elements and suggestions Existing, new or amended assets.
1	Homepage	Easily be able to locate and select the dresses category.	If users have been to the site before they want to get straight into the category listing, however in testing it was noted that users "may get side-tracked by other products on the homepage". New users will want to get a sense that the brand offers the types of clothes they would buy.	Images of the latest seasons clothing. Sale and offer information. Clear navigation into the product categories.
2	Category listing	Easily select a product they like the look of.	Colour, price and style are all necessary. An indication of available sizes is useful at this stage, but can be omitted as long as it's clear on the product page. "I just like looking through everything available and clicking through to the dresses I like."	Photos that show the front and back of garments: Price and discount information. Alternate color, if applicable
3	Product page	Add the dress to their basket.	Further images including details and model shots. Sizing and availability. Delivery and returns information. "I often buy two different sizes to try both, so I need to make sure it's easy to send the one I don't want back".	Large (fullscreen) photos both on and off models. Detailed sizing guide with stock levels for each size and color. Delivery and returns information. Quantity and add to basket. Product description including material, detailing information and the designer.

FIGURE 4: Content requirements. Ensuring your content aligns with the user requirements.

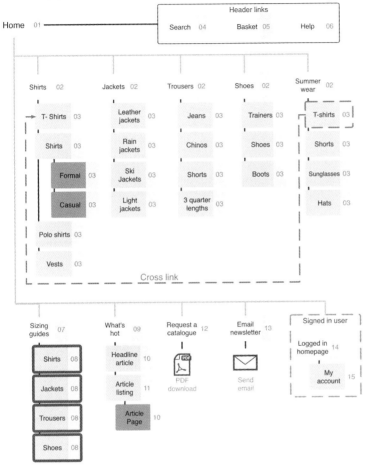

FIGURE 5: Sitemaps. Sorting out the structure, navigation, and labeling.

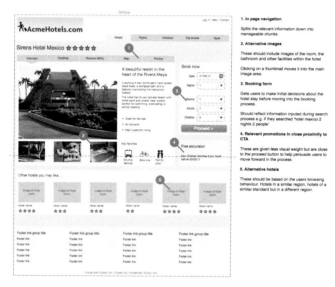

FIGURE 6: Wireframes. Prototyping, visualizing, and validating.

FIGURE 7: User testing reports. Seeing the world through your users' eyes and deciding what to focus on.

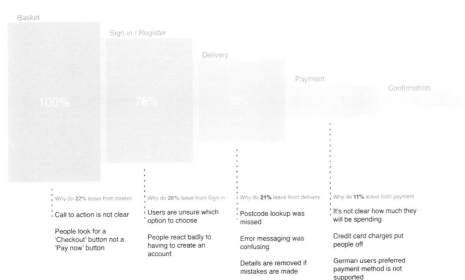

Why do 90% of people drop out of the checkout process?

FIGURE 8: Funnel diagrams. Analyzing and optimizing the user journey.

Putting the documents into context

The documents in this book can be used on their own or in tandem to inform a specific area of the user experience.

For example, let's say that you're working on maintaining an existing site but the team has lost focus of who the users are and what they need. Decisions are being made based on what the project team thinks the users want (this is not and never will be a user centered design process). Developing personas and task models would take the focus away from the project team and put it back on the user, helping to inform the short-term tactical projects and long-term strategic aims.

Alternatively you may be creating a product from scratch and able to put together a plan that incorporates several or all of the elements described in this book. To provide context, Figure 9 shows a typical project process, user experience activities, and documents produced. You'll notice the repetition of validation and benchmark testing throughout.

What are the business goals for the project?

Interviews and meetings held with the project and stakeholder teams to understand the projects objectives and how it will be measured.

Output: Summary of business requirements and key performance indicators (KPIs)

Business insight

User insight

What are the user needs from the project?

Observations and research with users to understand who they are and how they think. Analytics and search log review to understand existing patterns.

Output: Personas, task models, competitor benchmarking report

How to align the business and user needs?

Workshops with the project and stakeholder team to understand the research, discuss objectives and make the idea concrete through sketching and concept designs.

Output: Prioritised objectives, roll-out plan and visualizations

Vision definition

Design

How does the site feel and look to use?

Initially the focus is on the information architecture, content, user journeys, sketching and wireframes. Then on the application of the brand onto the design and validation of the chosen routes.

Output: User journey, content audit and strategy, sitemap, wireframes, validation testing reports

How does the site work?

Working with the developers and production team to help realise the user experience.

Output: User experience consultancy, validation testing reports

Develop

Measure & optimize

How do we measure and improve?

Analysis, testing and improvements on an ongoing basis to optimise the user experience and site performance.

Output: Funnel diagrams and analytics analysis, A/B and Multi Variant Testing testing, regular user testing

FIGURE 9: A typical project process.

> **note** All of the templates, stencils, and icons used in this book are available to download and use freely at http://cxpartners.com/resources.

Enjoy yourselves!

Facilitating and engaging in user-centered design projects is rewarding for you and the project team. You'll help people love the products and services you produce, and, in turn, those products and services will become more successful.

So, have fun with the techniques and Tweet us to let us know how you get on.

—Richard (@richardcaddick) and Steve (@steve_cable).

chapter 1

Personas

A PERSONA IS a document that describes the ways in which certain types of people will use your website. Usually one persona is created for each type of user. Personas are used to show you the goals that users will be trying to achieve on your website. See Figure 1-1.

In this chapter, you will learn exactly what information is needed to create a truly useful persona. You will learn the best time in which to produce your personas, what information needs to be communicated, and how to lay it out in a clear and concise way. You will also get some ideas on how to generate the information that is needed to create a solid persona that is based on real people.

FIGURE 1-1: A persona helps you understand users' goals when using your website.

What makes a good persona?

A good persona is based on real people and solid research. It focuses on the key goals that user groups have to achieve, user behaviors, and user attitudes while completing their goals.

Ultimately, personas need to help you understand if any decisions you make will help or hinder your users.

When to create a persona

To put it plainly, you should create one now. Unlike wireframes or prototypes, personas don't fit into a specific part of a single project process. Instead they help guide *every* part of every project. They provide a quick reference for design decisions, idea generation, and strategic changes.

Personas and task models sit closely alongside each other and are built on the same types of research, so for efficiency the two can be developed side-by-side—this also allows you to consider different personas based on the task models.

Personas should be living documents. They capture a snapshot of an audience at a specific time. As further research uncovers new insights, your personas need to be updated to reflect them. Doing so turns the personas into an ongoing strategic tool that constantly represents the user behavior and uncovers new opportunities.

What are you communicating?

A persona has two goals:

> To help you make design decisions.

> To remind you that real people will be using your system.

A good persona is not based on demographics or stories; it's based on the tasks, behaviors, and attitudes of your users. For example, if you're developing a vacation reservation site, your personas shouldn't focus on what newspapers users read, what cars they drive, and what the measurements of the inside of their legs are. This information doesn't help you develop your product. Avoid irrelevant information; focus on key goals. This helps you imagine how people will use your product—and that helps you make it more useful to them.

Use short descriptive bulleted points

Avoid stories. Don't get me wrong, I love stories, but not in personas. The problem with stories is it's difficult to write them well and people won't take the time to read them unless they are incredibly engaging. Keeping your persona content down to short sentences and bullets creates less effort for the reader.

Base personas on real people

Personas should be based on real people from real research. A good way to ensure this is to use somebody you met during your research as a base for your persona. Choose somebody who is a fair representation of the persona and then add in any other relevant pieces of information you found in your research. This means your persona shows a fair representation of the group it's representing but uses real examples that you have really experienced.

Use descriptive photography

Photos can be a really valuable part of a persona, but more often then not they are used really badly. Mostly photos are used to put a human face against the persona, so a cheesy smiling portrait is stuck at the top of it. Photos on personas can do much more than that.

The right photo can tell the reader something about this user group just from looking at it. For example if one of your personas has a hard time using technology, then the photo should be of someone struggling to use technology. Photos in your personas should reflect user behavior, not just age and gender.

Avoid using stock images. They are tacky and make your personas feel less real (real people don't stand in studios with cheesy grins). Ideally you want to use photos of real users who you encountered during ethnographical research (explained later in this chapter). Photos of real users performing relevant tasks will help ground your personas in reality. Of course this is not always possible. An alternative is to use an online photo sharing site like Flickr. These have a wealth of candid photos of real people in real situations. However, you need to be aware of the licensing that is associated with the images and may need to seek permission from the photographer before you use them.

Figure 1-2 shows an image from a persona for a shopping site.

A nice addition is to include a photo of the personas' environment. If you show the space that they inhabit while trying to use your system, you might come up with some interesting ideas of their behaviors and constraints. It could tell you if they work in a messy environment that is full of distractions. It could show you the kinds of devices they use: laptops or mobiles. It could show you any other resources they use to complete their goals: books, brochures, or notepads. Figure 1-3 shows an example environment image for a persona.

FIGURE 1-2: This example shows their clothes shopping behavior as functional (just buying socks and pants).

FIGURE 1-3: This is the actual desk of co-author Steve Cable. What's it tell you about his environment?

Anatomy of a persona

Here's a breakdown of what you need to include in your persona. Figure 1-4 shows examples of the concepts that follow.

Photos

Use representative photos that put a human face against the persona and also tell the reader something about the person behind the persona.

Persona names

A name humanizes the persona, but also makes it easy to know which you are referring to in design meetings: "This idea would work for Ken, but not so much for Deirdre."

User quotes

A quote from somebody you met during research can bring the persona to life and give a quick overview of that persona's state of mind when trying to complete her goals.

Key goals

If you know what people want do on your website or with your software, you can ensure you have everything in place to make sure they can do it. Different personas will have a different number of goals, but generally you want to know the answer to these questions:

> Do they have a specific task to complete quickly?

> Do they want to take their time and enjoy the experience?

> What do they need to know?

> What is their ultimate goal?

Behaviors

Knowing what motivates people and how they are likely to be feeling helps you create persuasive designs that will influence choices and help reduce any worries they may have. Look for answers to the following questions:

> What are their motivations for using the system?

> What are they likely to be feeling when they use your system? (Do they assume it's going to be a frustrating experience?)

> Do they have a lot of spare time to perform their tasks?

> What influences their choices?

> What puts them off or makes them lose trust?

Must dos

A *must do* is a simple description of what you need to do to support your users' key tasks and behaviors. These must be about your system or service as a whole because they can be used to validate any design decisions or new functionality.

Must nevers

A *must never* is the same as a must do, except it focuses on what you must avoid at all costs. Avoiding any of the points in your must never section will help prevent designing a system that will make your users feel lost or confused.

 Key goals

- Knows what he wants to buy
- Avoid spending time browsing
- Get something balanced between price and quality (look is not important)

✔ We must

- Clearly show key features
- Provide easy comparison between products
- Show him relevant offers

 Behaviours

- Gets bored shopping quickly
- Wants tried and tested products
- Happy to let others do the thinking for him
- Easily influenced by discounts

 We must never

- Don't focus on fluffy product descriptions
- Don't overwhelm him with choice

FIGURE 1-4: A completed persona that focuses on user goals and behaviors.

Who is the audience?

Personas are for anybody who needs to make a decision about the design of your system, or a decision about your strategy as a whole. A well-researched persona can help inform these decisions.

They are especially useful for companies that don't know anything about their customers. It gives you a chance to think about *why* you are doing *what* you are doing.

Experience shows that it's important to get buy-in from senior stakeholders when creating personas. This ensures they aren't forgotten and left to gather dust on the shelf. Getting buy-in does not mean showing the personas off once they are completed.

It's important to get senior stakeholders involved in the process early on. Invite them to research and testing sessions so they can see for themselves some of the behaviors and goals that will be presented in your personas. That way they will see where the content of the personas is coming from and believe in them more than if they were just slapped on their desk after six months of research behind closed doors.

Personas are also very useful for internal or external research teams. If any user research is being carried out, the persona is a very useful tool for recruiting test participants. Goal-based personas allow you to recruit users based on those goals. For example, when testing a travel website you will recruit users whose goal is to book a long holiday for a family, and some users whose goal it is to book a short break for a couple.

As shown in Figure 1-5, it's useful to keep personas readily available, or on constant display, to allow project teams to reference them when making design decisions.

FIGURE 1-5: A handy display of user personas.

How to validate personas

Personas are based on lots of research so initially they will not need validation. But as time goes on, you need to be sure your personas are still relevant.

For quick validation you can always run your personas past the customer service team or call center staff. These are the people who have the most contact with your users; they will be able to see if your personas ring true with what they experience, or just never happen.

Personas can also be validated against any other research that gets carried out for any other projects within your company. If you're performing some usability testing to find some quick wins or online surveys to gather customer experience information, you can evaluate the results with your personas. Comparing your results will show if new findings are consistent with your personas, making the personas still relevant. If the findings are inconsistent with your personas, then they may need updating. However at that point it would be safest to perform more specific validation research to be sure.

RESEARCH AND WORKSHOP IDEAS

The key to a good persona is research. Without that, personas are guaranteed to fail. Personas that are simply made up are easy to spot and are easily forgotten about.

Start with a theory

So you need to talk to lots of people, but who do you talk to? You don't have your personas yet to know what types of people use your system, right?

You need to start with a hypothesis. Theorize what the core goals are and recruit research participants based on those goals.

Base your theories on what your company already knows—no matter how little the information might be—about its customers or users. Think of what kinds of goals you assume they need to complete and what kinds of scenarios these people may be in. For example, if you're running research for a mother and baby retailer, don't just recruit based on goals like, "Needs to buy a crib," or "Needs to buy a stroller." Instead, recruit based on wider scenarios and goals, such as:

> First-time mother trying to buy everything she needs.

> Mother of two or more who needs to make a large necessary purchase.

> A relative looking for a gift for a mother.

Your goals must also cover all relevant aspects of the project.

Once you have a theory, carry out your research. Your research will either prove or disprove those theories.

> **tip** The more research you do, the more accurate and robust your personas become. This creates a trade-off between budget and quality. To have personas, you must do research, but a six-person usability test will not be enough.

The following sections provide a brief overview of some ways that you can gather information to create your personas.

RESEARCH TECHNIQUE: Listen in on call centers

If you have a call center available, it is a great resource for listening to the questions and needs of lots of users in a short space of time. However, you don't get the same level of information as depth interviews. The idea is to listen in and not interact. Note what people are calling for, the questions they have, and the information they need. By the end of the day you should see patterns and themes emerging. If we use the mother and baby retailer example, then you will want to listen for:

> The types of products they're trying to buy.

> The information they want to know about the products.

> The problems they face when trying to buy those products.

You can do call center listening remotely by dialing in, but it's much more beneficial to go to the call center in person (see Figure 1-6). This allows you to talk to the call center staff. That's important because they are going to know the most common problems that callers have and the most common questions asked. Hopefully this will ring true with what you have been hearing and seeing in other research. You can also learn the solutions that call center staff provide to people.

Specifically, you want to find out the following information from the call center staff:

> What are the most common problems or complaints?

> What are the solutions you give to people?

FIGURE 1-6: Listening in on calls between customers and call center staff can quickly uncover common issues and user goals.

RESEARCH TECHNIQUE: Conduct depth interviews

Depth interviews allow you to speak to only a small number of people, but as the name suggests, you can gather some in-depth information.

The idea is to get users to talk to you about their previous experiences when trying to complete goals relevant to your system. You need to talk to the theorized groups of users you initially defined (for example, first-time mother, mother of two or more, and somebody buying a gift for a mother). Discuss what they remember from the last time they completed their goal. In particular you want to know:

> What information did they need to know?

> What problems did they encounter?

> What were they able/unable to do?

> What tasks were involved in achieving their goal?

> What did they use to achieve their goal (websites, books, other people, for instance)?

> If they were going to attempt to achieve that goal again, how would they do it?

The rich, qualitative information you gather will give you an idea of the kinds of themes that may go into your persona, but because the numbers are small you may need to use other techniques to get more results to validate those themes.

RESEARCH TECHNIQUE: Conduct ethnographic research

What we mean by *ethnographic research* is simply watching (and talking to) people trying to achieve their goals in their natural environment (for example, an in-depth interview in their natural environment).

We once did some research for eBay, trying to understand the goals and needs of users who sold the most stuff on the site. Rather than getting them into the lab, we went to their homes. This meant we could see the type of environment they worked in, which helped build an idea of any constraints they might have. We also could be shown things, rather than just talk about things—like what they were currently trying to sell and how they went about trying to describe it on eBay.

For the mother and baby retailer, a good place to do an ethnographic study is in their stores (with permission from the company, of course). Subtly follow customers in order to see what they are buying (if anything). Listen to conversations they have with shop staff. This can help you understand customers' decision processes. It's also a good idea to talk to the store staff at the end of the day about what you have discovered. This will help validate your findings and draw out more stories about customer behavior.

Ethnographic research is great for getting a good depth of information from a small number of people. You also learn many things from people in their natural spaces that you wouldn't in a lab environment.

WORKSHOP IDEA: Define your personas

By this point you will have recruited participants based on the goals you identified for using your system. You will have spoken to them about how they perform those goals and discovered the behaviors they use. Now you need to take this information and group it into personas.

Take the notes from the individuals you have interviewed and cluster them by the goals set during recruitment. For example, group all the people who were recruited because they were first time mothers trying to buy everything they need and group all the people who were purchasing gifts for mothers.

Focusing on one group at a time, look at the different approaches people took to completing the goals you set. You may see that everybody went about completing the goal in the same way. However, you may often find that different people approach the same goal in different ways and may even have different goals. For example, buying clothes may split into those people who relish the opportunity and enjoy the process, and those people who buy clothes for necessity only—two very different approaches to the same goal.

Once you have your final list of personas, you need to determine their behaviors. Go through the notes for each persona at a time, pick out the interesting behaviors, write them onto Post-Its, stick the Post-Its up on a wall (see Figure 1-7), and group the interesting behaviors that appear frequently. It is a good idea to base your personas on one specific participant and enrich it with the findings from others.

Determining must dos and must-nevers is left until last because they are based on the key goals and behaviors. You need to think about how you can help this user and how you can avoid frustrating and confusing him. Remember to not be too specific. If you include a must do such as, "Must use red on the call to action on the product page," that will help only with a specific decision. These rules must be broad enough to help with decisions across the whole site, system, or even the business. For example, "Must never overwhelm the user with choice."

FIGURE 1-7: Using Post-Its to group interesting behaviors helps to show common themes from your research.

What's the simplest way to create a persona?

The actual design of the persona document should be pretty simple anyway. What really counts is the quality of the data that sits behind it. If you are really pressed for time or need to get a brief preview out ahead of the final document, here is a quick way of presenting personas using Microsoft Word.

Persona images

The best way to save time and effort is to use alternatives to photos. If you didn't collect appropriate photos during research, sourcing ones that are good enough can be time consuming and difficult. As an alternative, you could use icons to represent each persona. This isn't as personal as a photo, but at least each persona will be easily distinguishable when all are stuck up on the wall.

Document titles

Use the persona name as the document title. It's always a good idea to use the name of a participant you met during research to keep it realistic. (Also, you'll find you will get hung up on selecting a name.) Use a large font (48 points) so it can be easily read when stuck on a wall.

Use a quote from the user as a subtitle. Make the font size smaller than your title (22 points). This is a supporting piece of information, so give it less emphasis than everything else by making the font a lighter shade of gray. Use italics and quotation marks to make it clear that this is a user quote.

Subheadings

Create a subheading for each of the key areas of information (Key Goals, Behaviors, Must Do, Must Never). Use a smaller font again (18 points).

Bulleted lists

Use bulleted lists to display the information in each section. This is both an easier way to write and an easier way to read. To create a bulleted list, write each point on its own line. Highlight the text you want to make in to bullets and in the top menu select the Home tab, then click on Bullets. From here you can choose what style of bulleted list you want. It's best to avoid numbered lists for your bullets unless the points you are making have some kind of prioritization. If you want to tweak the line spacing between each point, highlight the bulleted text, right-click it, and select Paragraph. You can edit the Line spacing options in the window that pops up.

Figure 1-8 shows a persona created in Word.

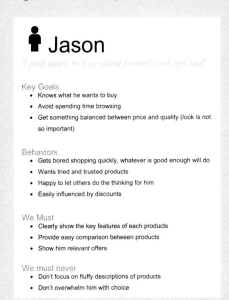

Jason

'I just want to buy what I need and get out'

Key Goals
- Knows what he wants to buy
- Avoid spending time browsing
- Get something balanced between price and quality (look is not so important)

Behaviors
- Gets bored shopping quickly, whatever is good enough will do
- Wants tried and trusted products
- Happy to let others do the thinking for him
- Easily influenced by discounts

We Must
- Clearly show the key features of each products
- Provide easy comparison between products
- Show him *relevant* offers

We must never
- Don't focus on fluffy descriptions of products
- Don't overwhelm him with choice

FIGURE 1-8: If you're short on time, you can use Word to create a persona.

HOW TO Create personas in PowerPoint

This section shows you how to create a persona layout that you can reuse for each of the personas you create. The instructions describe how to create the personas in PowerPoint 2010.

note Mac users can either use the Mac version of PowerPoint or skip to the OmniGraffle tutorial, which shows how to create the same document.

Creating and setting up the slide presentation

To create a new slide presentation and set it up correctly, follow these steps:

1 Go to the File tab and click New. A menu of document templates and themes is displayed.

2 The Blank presentation should be highlighted by default. (If not, click it.) Click the Create button on the right (see Figure 1-9).

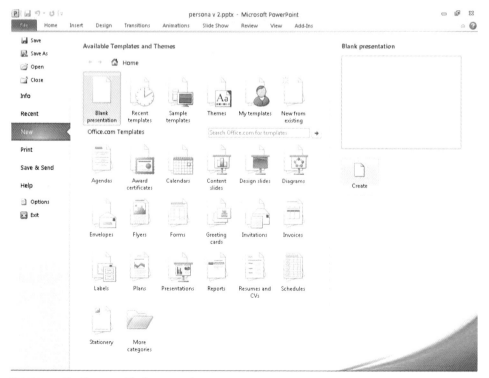

FIGURE 1-9: Creating a new Blank presentation.

The default presentation uses a landscape layout. The persona design uses a portrait layout, so you need to change this setting.

3 Go to the Design tab and in the Page Setup group, click Slide Orientation and then choose Portrait.

4 Go to the View tab and in the Show group, select the Guides option.

When Guides is enabled, the page is divided both horizontally and vertically. This will help divide the page vertically to give equal space to both the persona image and the persona information.

5 On the Power Point slide, select the Click to add title box and delete it.

6 Click to add subtitle box and delete it as well.

caution Make sure you delete the text boxes, not just the text that sits within them.

Adding persona images and titles

This section describes how to add images into your persona, how to resize images, and how to create the page titles.

Inserting an image

To insert the persona image:

1 Go to the Insert tab and click the Picture button.

2 Select the image you want and then click Open.

3 Click the blue corner points of the image to resize it, making sure you hold down the Shift key as you resize the image. This retains the same aspect ratio and ensures the sizing isn't warped.

4 Drag the corners of your image to resize and position your image so it takes up the top half of the page and the person in the photo is over to the left or right of the slide. This means you will have you will have space on the opposite side to overlay a title.

note Don't worry if your image spills over into the bottom of the page. You can crop it to stop this from happening.

❺ To crop the image, select the image and then in the Picture Tools Format tab, select Crop (see Figure 1-10). The controls around the edge of the image will change.

❻ Drag the black lines on the edge of the image to crop it. They should snap to the edges of the page and the guidelines.

❼ Once you're happy with your crop, just deselect the image.

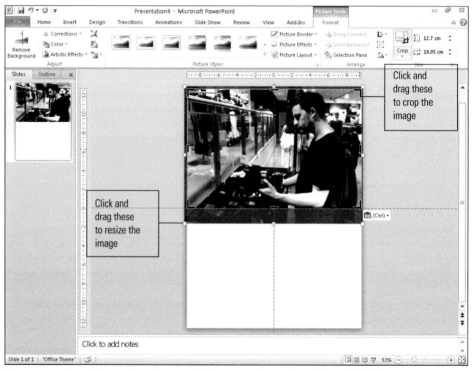

FIGURE 1-10: Use resizing and cropping to make the persona image take up the top half of the page.

Adding an overlay color

Before you add the document title, add a transparent block of color over part of the image to make the text more readable.

❶ In the Home tab, select a rectangle from the shapes menu and draw a rectangle over the top of your image.

❷ With the shape selected, go to the Shape Fill drop-down, select Gradient, and then choose More Gradients.

❸ From the Fill menu, select Gradient fill. Set the following (see Figure 1-11):

- Type drop-down: Linear

- Gradient stops: white (select each and choose white from the Color menu below)

- Transparency of right stop: 100%

- Transparency of left stop: 20%

- Transparency of middle stop: 20%

❹ Click Close when you're finished.

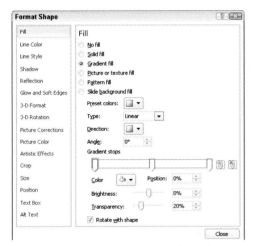

FIGURE 1-11: Adding a transparent overlay to the image.

Inserting a title

To insert a title, follow these steps:

❶ Click the Insert tab and in the Illustrations group, click the Shapes down arrow.

❷ In the Recently Used Shapes category, click the text box.

❸ Click wherever you want to type.

❹ Use your personas name as the document title.

❺ Make the title large (60 points). Use a font that is easy to read, such as Arial.

note   Your personas are likely to be viewed as PDFs. If you use a font that is specific to a Mac or specific to a PC, a user who isn't using the right operating system might have difficulty reading the font.

6 Change the font color to a dark gray and position the text box in the top corner of the page over your gradient.

7 Repeat Steps 5 and 6 to add your user quote except this time use a smaller font (28 points) and use italics and quote marks to make it clear that it's a quote.

See Figure 1-12. Play around with the size and position of your titles to see what looks good against the background image.

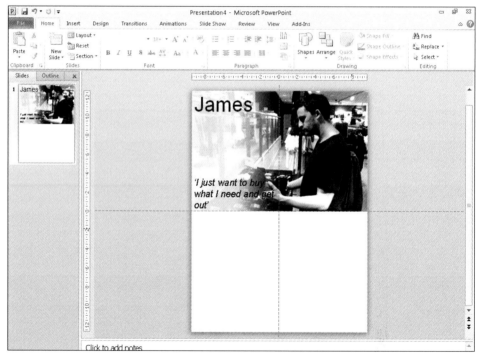

FIGURE 1-12: Place your title and subtitle over the transparent overlay.

Adding icons, subheadings, and bulleted lists

Each group of information in the persona (for example, Key Goals) will need an icon to illustrate each group of information, a clear subheading, and a bulleted list to display the information. Use the same positions for subheadings and icons across all your personas; this will simplify the comparison of each persona.

Inserting icons

The icons should be the same size, fairly small, and a light gray. They should illustrate the heading but should not take attention away from more relevant information.

❶ Go to the Insert tab and click the Picture button.

❷ Select the icons you want and click open. When all the icons have been added to the slide, select them all.

❸ Resize them by going to the Picture Tools format tab and using the size controls on the right of the menu. Set all the icons to 1.5 cm by 1.5 cm (see Figure 1-13).

❹ To change the icons to a lighter gray, select one and in the Adjust group, click the Corrections menu.

❺ Select the Picture correction options and reduce the contrast by 100%.

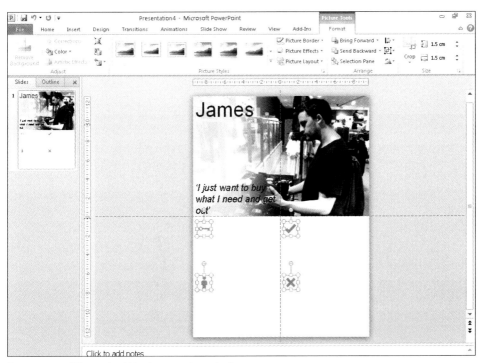

FIGURE 1-13: All icons should be the same size and color.

Adding subheadings

Now add the titles for each section of information:

❶ Make the font size 24 points and change the color to a light gray to match the icons (see Figure 1-14).

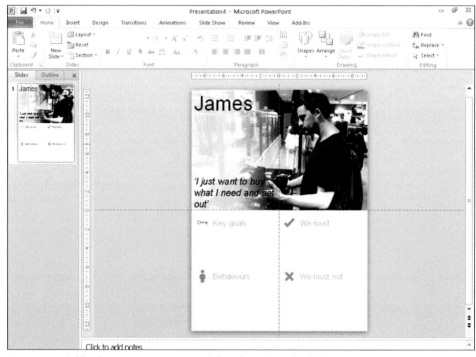

FIGURE 1-14: Subheadings are set to 24 point and the color is changed to light gray.

❷ To make sure the icons and titles are all aligned nicely, click the Home tab and in the Drawing group, click Arrange and choose Align.

Adding bulleted lists

Use bulleted lists for the main pieces of information. That makes the information much quicker and easier to read. To create a bulleted list, follow these steps:

❶ Create a text box.

❷ Type your information into the text box.

❸ Select all of the text in the box.

❹ Click the Home tab and in the Paragraph group, click the Bullets button and choose round bullet points (see Figure 1-15).

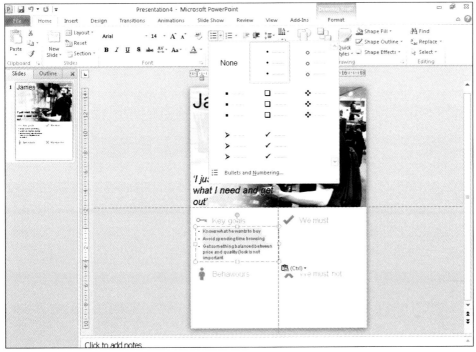

FIGURE 1-15: The round bullet points are simple yet also effective at helping each point stand out visually.

You can adjust the distance between the bullets and the text by clicking into the text box and dragging the markers on the rulers at the top of the page. It's also a good idea to increase the line spacing to make each point more readable:

❶ Select the text box and click the Home tab.

❷ In the Paragraph group, click the Line Spacing button and then click Line Spacing Options (see Figure 1-16).

❸ In the Spacing group, change the After setting to 6 pt.

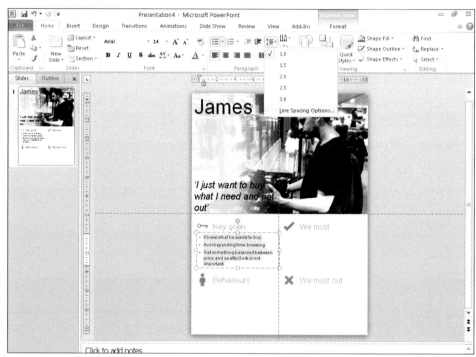

FIGURE 1-16: The line spacing options give you more control over the space between bullet points.

Make the font around 14 points depending on how much text you need to fit in. Change the color to a darker gray than all the other text because these are the most important pieces of information.

For each of your subsequent personas, just duplicate this page by right-clicking the slide in the preview panel on the left and clicking Duplicate Slide (see Figure 1-17). You just need to change the photo and all the necessary text. It's best to leave as many elements as possible in the same place to make all the personas consistent.

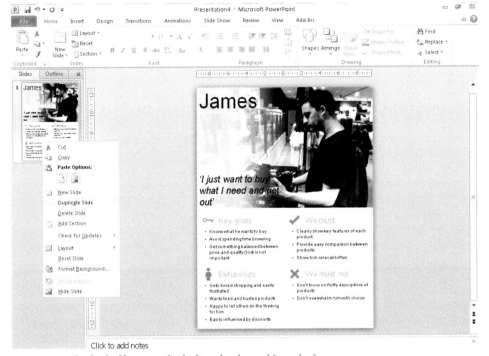

FIGURE 1-17: The finished layout can be duplicated and reused for each of your personas.

HOW TO ## Create personas in OmniGraffle Pro

This section explains how to create a persona using OmniGraffle Pro. You will learn how to set up the document and add all the necessary images and text elements to create a persona template that can be reused for all the personas you create.

Creating and setting up the presentation

To create a new presentation and set it up correctly, follow these steps:

❶ Go to the File menu, click New, and then select the blank document from the template chooser.

❷ Go to File and choose Page Setup.

❸ For the Paper Size setting, select A4 (see Figure 1-18).

❹ For the Orientation setting, choose Portrait.

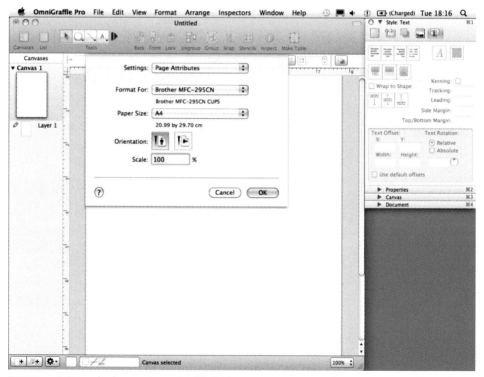

FIGURE 1-18: Set up the document as a printable size because most personas exist as print outs stuck on walls.

Finally, you want to set some guides up that run down the center of the Canvas horizontally and vertically. This helps you line all your information up and provides you with equal space to the persona image and the persona details.

5 Go to the View menu and make sure Rulers and Guides are turned on. They should be enabled by default.

6 Set your guidelines to 280 px horizontally and 390 px vertically (see Figure 1-19).

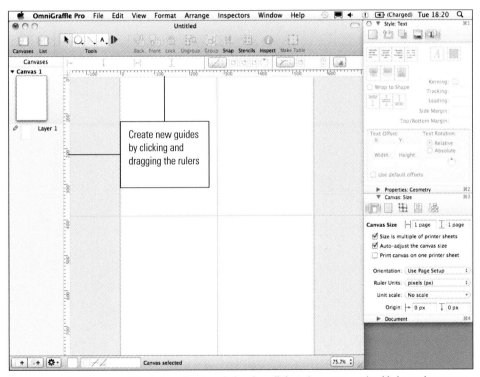

FIGURE 1-19: Setting your guides to these locations helps align all the information as it's added into the persona.

Adding persona images and titles

This section explains how to add and resize images as well as how to add the titles and subtitles.

Inserting an image

To add images into OmniGraffle, simply drag them from the finder window onto the canvas.

Once you have placed your persona photo onto the canvas you will need to resize and crop it to so it takes up the top half of the page. Here's the best way to do that:

❶ Select the image and, in the image section of the inspector, click the Natural size button (see Figure 1-20). This masks the image allowing you to determine the area you want your image to take up and easily crop it to fit.

❷ With Natural size selected, resize the border around the image so it covers the top half of the page, and then use the Size slider in the inspector to resize the image to fill the space.

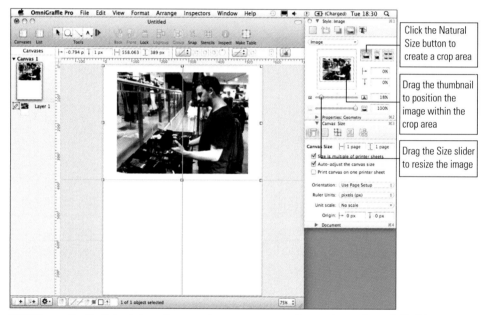

FIGURE 1-20: Use the Natural size options to make sure your persona image takes up the top half of the page.

note It's a good idea to make sure the person in the photo is over to the left or right of the image. This means you will have space on the opposite side to overlay a title.

Adding an overlay color

Before you add the title to the image, add an overlay color to make any text that sits on the image more readable:

❶ Draw a rectangle over the half of the image that doesn't have the person in it

❷ Open the stroke options in the style section of the inspector and uncheck the Stroke checkbox (the line around the shape).

❸ Open the shadow options in the style section of the inspector and uncheck the Shadow checkbox.

❹ Open the fill options in the style section of the inspector. Click the Fill type drop-down and change the Fill type to Double Linear Blend. Use the Angle text box to change the angle of the gradient to 0 degrees.

❺ Click the color boxes on the right of the inspector to change all three colors in the gradient to white; change the Opacity of the top two to 80% and the bottom one to 0%.

❻ Drag the slider next to the gradient colors in the inspector down a fraction to make the lighter part of the rectangle stand out a little more. See Figure 1-21.

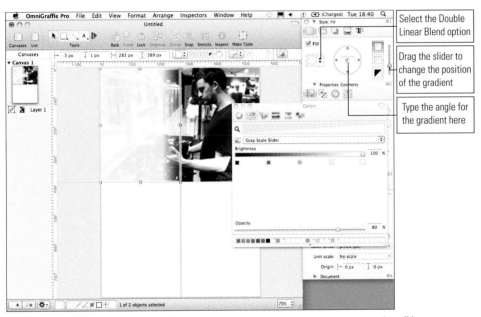

FIGURE 1-21: Adding a transparent overlay on your image means any text you put on top of it will be more readable.

Inserting a title

Next, add the persona name and quote. It's best to use the name as the title of the page and the quote as a subtitle. Add a text box over the gradient and use a large font (around 64 points) for the title. For the quote, use a smaller font in italics and quote marks. Play around with the size and position of your titles to see what looks good against the background image. See Figure 1-22.

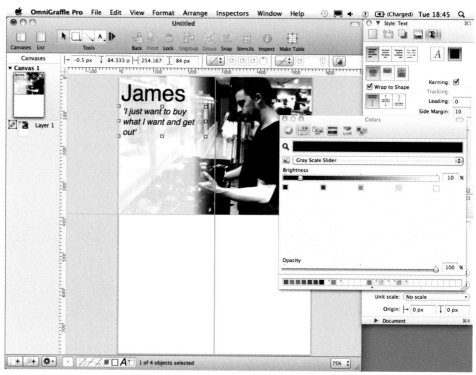

FIGURE 1-22: Place your title and subtitle over the transparent overlay.

Adding subheadings and bulleted lists

Each group of information in the persona (for example, Key Goals) will need an icon to illustrate each group of information, a clear subheading, and a bulleted list to display the information. Use the same positions for subheadings and icons across all your personas; this will simplify the comparison of each persona.

Inserting icons

The icons should be the same size, fairly small, and a light gray. They should illustrate the heading but should not take attention away from more relevant information.

> **note** The icons used in this example are available to download along with many others from the book's supporting website at http://cxpartners.co.uk/resources.

➊ When all the icons have been added to the document, select them all.

➋ Resize them by going to the Properties: Geometry section of the inspector and changing the height and width to 50 px (see Figure 1-23).

➌ To gray the icons, open the Style: Image section of the inspector and reduce opacity to 50%.

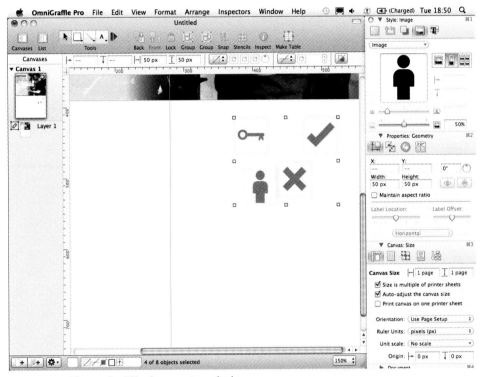

FIGURE 1-23: All icons should be the same size and color.

Adding subheadings

Now add the titles for each section of information:

➊ Make the font size 24 points and change the color to a light gray to match the icons.

➋ Make sure the icons and titles are all aligned nicely by opening the Canvas: Alignment section (see Figure 1-24) and aligning the icons horizontally with the titles.

FIGURE 1-24: Align the icons horizontally with the titles.

Adding bulleted lists

Use bulleted lists for the main pieces of information. This makes the information much quicker and easier to read. To create a bulleted list:

1 Create a text box.

2 Type your information into the text box.

3 Select all the text.

4 Click the Lists drop-down menu at the top of the canvas and select the round bullet style (see Figure 1-25).

You can adjust the distance between the bullet and the text by selecting all the text and dragging the arrows in the rulers at the top of the canvas (also refer to Figure 1-25).

With the text selected, drag these arrows to adjust the indent of the text

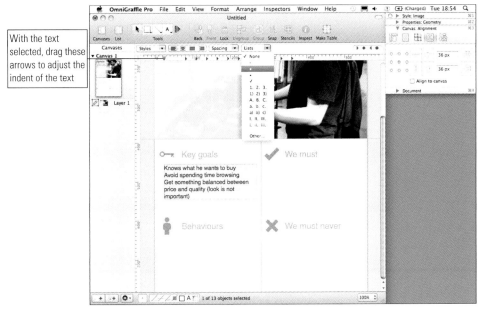

FIGURE 1-25: Selecting the round bullet style and adjusting indents.

It's a good idea to adjust the line spacing between the bullets to make everything easier to read:

❶ Select all the text and click the Spacing drop-down menu.

❷ Click Other.

❸ Adjust the Paragraph spacing after setting to 6.0 points (see Figure 1-26).

For each of your subsequent personas, just duplicate this page by right-clicking the slide in the canvas list panel on the left and clicking Duplicate Canvas (see Figure 1-27). You just need to change the photo and all the necessary text. It's best to leave as many elements as possible in the same place to make all the personas consistent.

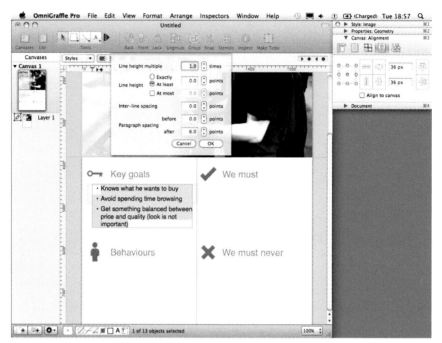

FIGURE 1-26: Use the Paragraph spacing after settings to keep the text aligned to the top of the text box.

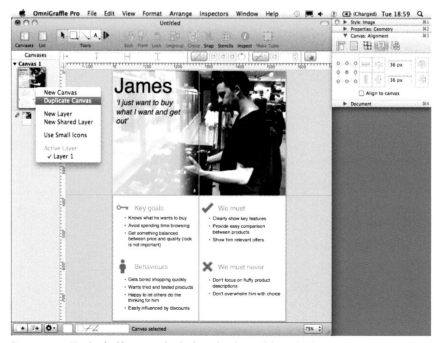

FIGURE 1-27: The finished layout can be duplicated and reused for each of your personas.

chapter 2

Task Models

A WELL-RESEARCHED TASK model will transform your project. It's the most important design deliverable, and for good reason — it shows what users do, the behavior they adopt, and specific requirements at each stage. Building a product or service around these findings is more successful because things happen when a user wants them to and the information they are after can be found.

It's also a vision document that identifies and communicates how a system needs to behave to match user expectations. It gives focus and direction to the experience you need to create—either in one go or upgrading piece by piece. See Figure 2-1.

FIGURE 2-1: A typical task model shows the steps users need to go through and the behavior they adopt in order to complete goals.

What makes a good task model?

At its most basic, a task model shows what tasks a user needs and expects to do to complete a goal. This can be enhanced with rich information such as behavior patterns, content requirements, the people involved, the media types that are being referenced, and the users' emotions.

Many well-financed projects have failed because they were designed without knowledge of the expected or desired user behavior. A task model ensures this doesn't happen by focusing the team on how the user behaves and what information he needs to complete his goal.

When to create a task model

If a task model hasn't been created, then there's no guarantee that the project you are working on will be a success. For that reason a task model should be created for every project.

Personas and task models sit alongside each other and feed off the same types of research, so for efficiency the two can be developed side by side, which also allows you to consider different task models based on the personas. Competitor benchmarking, personas, and task models are often covered in the same workshop because they usefully feed off each other.

Task models should be living documents. They capture a snapshot of an audience at a specific time, so they need to be refined and improved as future research uncovers new insights. Doing so turns them into an ongoing strategic tool that constantly represents the user behavior and uncovers opportunity. See Figure 2-2.

What are you communicating?

A task model (see Figure 2-3) tells a story about your audience that becomes a reference point throughout the projects design and development. The elements included are there to help you design solutions based on what people actually do.

FIGURE 2-2: Task models are rich documents that you can use to share stories about your users and open discussions on how best to design to meet their needs.

Goal: To find the perfect romantic city break

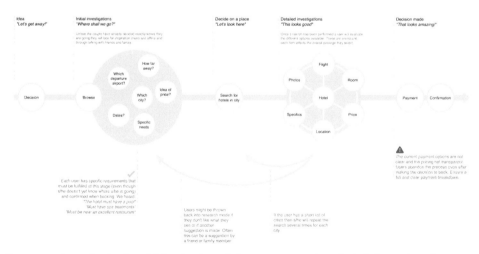

FIGURE 2-3: A completed task model showing the goal, the stages users go through, the behavior they adopt at each stage, and comments that identify the problems that need to be fixed.

The goal

What is it that the user is ultimately trying to do? For example, the user is looking to book a vacation.

The order of tasks

The flow of tasks to complete a goal gives the task model its overall shape. For larger tasks, these can be grouped into phases. For example, this could be from the initial investigations of where to go on vacation, the comparing of specific locations, and on to the actual booking of the vacation.

User behavior

User behavior shows how a user will want to move between each task. There are commonly three behavior states:

> **Direct connection.** One task leads on to the next. For example, a user has completed their holiday booking, clicked the submit button, and a confirmation page appears. See Figure 2-4.

FIGURE 2-4: An example of a direct connection: one step leads to the next without deviation.

warning Using direct connections where users don't want them will lead to a frustrating experience—they will feel that they are being forced down blind alleys without wanting to be.

> **Controlled evaluation.** A user wants to explore aspects of a well-defined product or service. For example, let's say you are buying a car and want to evaluate combinations of different wheels, engines, trims, and options (see Figure 2-5). The interface and navigation can focus just on allowing you to do these things in a controlled environment until you reach an outcome.

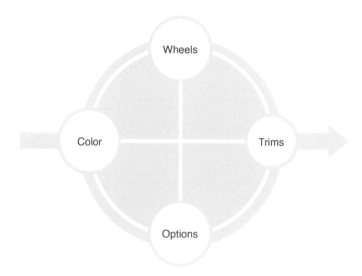

FIGURE 2-5: In a controlled evaluation, users move between known variables in order to make decisions. The designed interface should be focused on clearly presenting these elements.

> **Complex evaluation.** Complex evaluations can be found in almost every project. This is where a user requires several different, and often unrelated, needs to be fulfilled to complete a goal. When booking a vacation, for example, users evaluate dates, locations, activities, and cost. It is likely that they will have some specific requirements (such as *it must have a swimming pool* or *it must not be too close to a main road*). Their ultimate emotional goals might be to have a relaxing break. Uncovering and understanding this information gives guidance to how information is displayed, the feel you want to convey, and the deeper content that needs to be available. See Figure 2-6.

Emotional needs

What's driving the user behavior? Is it a need to understand, or a need to be reassured about the suitability of what he's looking at? For example, if he is buying a car, the exact specification might be less important than what the car will say about him to his friends and neighbors.

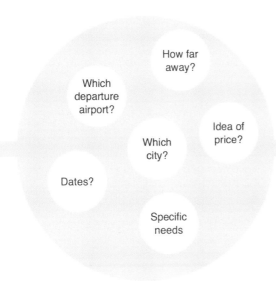

FIGURE 2-6: A complex evaluation recognizes the need to allow users to freely explore often unrelated variables in order to help them make decisions.

Who or what are they interacting with?

Are there other users involved and what other channels do they want to get the information from? In the example of choosing a vacation, we envision users reaching decisions collectively with friends or family members. They will use brochures and they will contact travel agents in order to explore their options.

Content requirements

Through research you will uncover what content needs users have at different times in their journey. This will range from the general information that every user has to the very specific content that a subset of the audience has. It's worth appreciating that if the specific needs aren't fulfilled, the task will fail for those users—or they will switch channels (for example, they'll leave a website in favor of picking up the phone to call a call center).

> **note** Refer to Chapter 4, "Content Requirements," for a simple way to collate these.

Existing barriers

If you have carried out some benchmark research it might be possible to identify the existing barriers and gaps (through lack of content or functionality) on the task model. Alternatively if the current model is drastically different from the proposed one, you can illustrate the two alongside each other.

Suggesting solutions

Where barriers have been identified and clear solutions exist, these can be overlaid as suggestions onto the task model and discussed in workshops with the project team.

The anatomy of a task model

Task models contain content and design information. This makes them more useful documents for the project team – ensuring that they are actionable. Visually the task model needs to be clear and the information expressed simply. So focus on conveying the most important elements. Figure 2-7 shows a task model that rather simply conveys detailed user behavior.

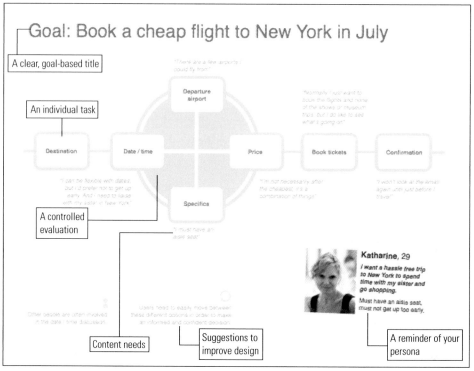

FIGURE 2-7: A simple task model showing the behavior a user adopts for booking a flight. Quotes relating to the persona reinforce what the user is doing at each stage.

Goal

What is the ultimate thing that the user is trying to do? Make this the title of the model.

Tasks

What are the individual things a user has to do to complete the goal? These become the individual elements.

Task phases

Show how the tasks group into natural phases of research, configuration or purchase.

User behavior

What are the behavior patterns a user goes through to complete a task? This is shown in the layout of the individual tasks and how they are connected.

Content needs

What information do users need to support the task? This is added as a note associated to a task.

Barriers

Where are the existing barriers and failure points of which you need to be aware of? Highlight these using an exclamation mark icon, as shown in Figure 2-3.

Design suggestions

What should the site do to help support the task? Include suggestions to discuss with the project team.

Personas

A reminder of the personas could be added to the task model, especially where different task models are developed to create different user scenarios.

Who is the audience?

Task models help to cut through potential complexity on projects. Involve the following teams in the data analysis workshop so they understand first hand how users think and what they do.

A broad audience should review and have input to the development of the task model:

> **Stakeholder team.** The task model is a great vision document. As you describe the user behavior you begin to unpack the user experience you want people to have on the site. It can help to cut through individual thoughts on what the right solution might be and encourage dialog around finding the best user experience.

> **Design team** (including user experience teams). Understanding the user behaviors uncovered in the task models provides insight into how the interface and flow should be designed.

> **Development team** (front- and back-end developers, business analysts). These are the people who can make the required functionality of the task model a reality. Work with them to ensure that the right data is available at the right time for users.

How to validate

A task model comes out of research, so in the short term it will not need validating per se. Any sitemaps, wireframes, designs, and, of course, the finished product will require validation through user testing. This testing is a good opportunity to refine your task model. See Figure 2-8.

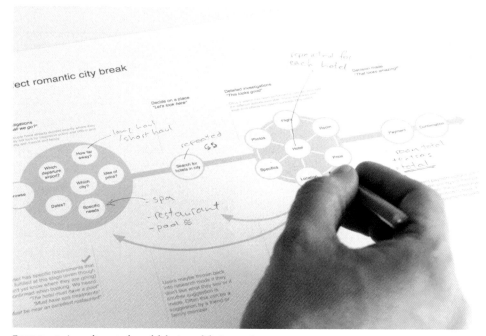

FIGURE 2-8: Amending a task model during validation testing.

When testing, remember to ask what users will expect to happen next and what they want to be able to do. If what they are expecting or what they want is different from what you've designed, there's a strong likelihood that your task model needs refining.

When you have a good task model you will be validating labeling and clarity of layout rather than the underlying flow and functionality.

RESEARCH AND WORKSHOP IDEAS

There are brilliant research techniques (such as structured depth interviews) where you can focus on the details of a user recalling a story. And there are methods (such as ethnography and diary studies) where you see the completion of tasks over a period of time. In this section, we've focused on some simple research techniques that you can easily slot into even the smallest of projects.

RESEARCH TECHNIQUE: Conduct research

You can (and should) do lightweight research on every project. Here are some ideas. In all approaches, jot down stories showing the people that users spoke to, the order in which users did things, the information users were after, and how they got it.

Visit call centers

If the organization you are working for has a call center, that's a perfect place to carry out research. Sit alongside an operator (it's good to partner with a few over the course of a day), listen in on as many calls as you can, and capture the user stories, noting:

> What do they ask for?

> In what order?

> How does the operator respond?

> Does the operator have additional reference content to hand?

> Is the call successful?

> What are the parting shots?

Make contextual observations

Customer service points, sales desks, and employee shadowing (following someone around for a period of time) are all perfect for seeing interactions between customers and businesses.

You are listening for the same information that you are in the call center but you also will observe the physical gestures and expressions that people make.

You'll need to think through how you take notes so as not to look too much like a researcher with a clipboard. Sneaking away to write notes after each customer interaction can work, but you might miss another good story. Audio recordings are good, but you'll most likely need permission.

Taking photos (see Figure 2-9) will remind you of the environment and act as prompts to help you recall stories. For example, in a clothing store, take photos that show the way in which people move around. Note how they initially scan all the items before selecting a few items to try on and eventually purchasing an item.

FIGURE 2-9: Photos help to remind you of environments and enable you to recall stories about user behavior.

Visit online forums

Forums are an ideal place to uncover user stories. You can sift through hundreds of posts in a relatively short amount of time and get a very clear sense of questions and expectations for any given task.

WORKSHOP IDEA: Analyze data

Once you've collected the research, you need to make sense of the stories and uncover user needs and behavior. Use Post-it Notes and a large whiteboard to position the individual elements and connect them with arrows.

You might discover that your personas have different task models—they might be trying to complete different goals or they might have significantly different ways of completing the same goal. In this instance, create a unique task model for each persona. Being able to compare the differences will show you how the product or service must support the needs of each user type.

Identify the goal

What is it that users ultimately want to do? Identifying the goal is key.

Analyze the information

Analyze each of the stories that you've collected and pull out the unique needs, associated content, and how people were looking to access the information. Put each unique need onto a Post-it Note.

Group the information

Group the Post-it Notes into the phases that users go through. Order the groups and give each a name (for example, for a commerce scenario, it might be research, purchase, and post-purchase). See Figure 2-10.

FIGURE 2-10: Signs of a good data analysis workshop. Unique needs have been identified and grouped into stages.

Identify the user behavior

Which behavior pattern are users using? Are they going straight from one task to the next or are they using controlled or complex evaluations to weigh the different elements?

Highlight the emotions

Finally run back through your stories and identify the users' emotional needs. What do they enjoy, what do they find frustrating? By understanding these, you can start to add a color and richness to your task model—and this helps you to prioritize the existing barriers that need to be resolved. Stick a red dot on Post-it Notes that identify pain points and a green dot on the positives.

What's the simplest way to illustrate a task model?

Once you complete the data analysis workshop, you'll have a whiteboard of Post-it Notes arranged into the task model and joined by arrows. This can be photographed, shared, and talked through with the project team immediately.

An alternative approach is to quickly sketch out the task model as in Figure 2-11 and share. Focus on the tasks and behavior states first to get the basic structure. Then overlay the richer content information and notes on top of that.

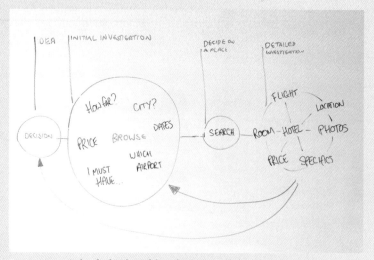

FIGURE 2-11. A sketched task model can be drawn and shared quickly with the project team.

You can create short stories of an individual's task process. Highlight what she was after and the way in which she went about getting it (see Figure 2-12). Putting several stories together can be a powerful way to communicate the diversity (and richness) of approaches that users take to complete the same task.

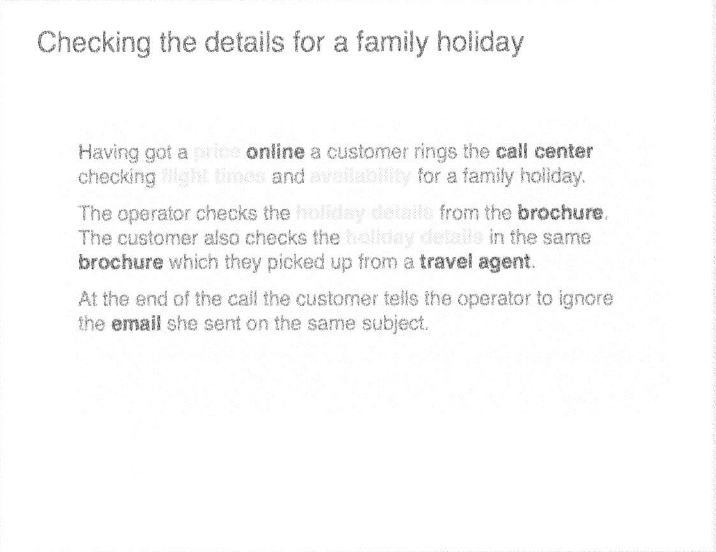

Checking the details for a family holiday

Having got a price **online** a customer rings the **call center** checking flight times and availability for a family holiday.

The operator checks the holiday details from the **brochure**. The customer also checks the holiday details in the same **brochure** which they picked up from a **travel agent**.

At the end of the call the customer tells the operator to ignore the **email** she sent on the same subject.

Figure 2-12 This story shows richness in the way a person clarified the details of a vacation she was interested in.

HOW TO Create task models in OmniGraffle

OmniGraffle is the perfect tool for creating task models. It's flexible enough to allow you to do some attractive information design but provides you with all the basic pre-defined shapes you'll need to pull it together simply.

Setting up the template

To set up the template, follow these steps:

❶ Launch OmniGraffle. The default templates are displayed.

❷ Select the blank template and click the New Diagram button.

The size of the canvas you use depends on the size and complexity of the task model you need to represent. Working on a large canvas is generally easier, as it gives you more room by default to position shapes—using A3 dimensions (297 mm by 420 mm) is a good starting point.

To change the canvas size:

❶ Go to the File menu and choose Page Setup.

❷ Click the Paper Size drop down and select Manage Custom Sizes to enter your own dimensions.

❸ Click the + button, give the custom size a name (in this case, A3), and then type the required dimensions.

❹ Click OK in this dialog box and then click OK in the Page Setup dialog box to set the new canvas size (see Figure 2-13).

> **tip** Additional canvas controls can be accessed by clicking the Inspect button shown in Figure 2-13.

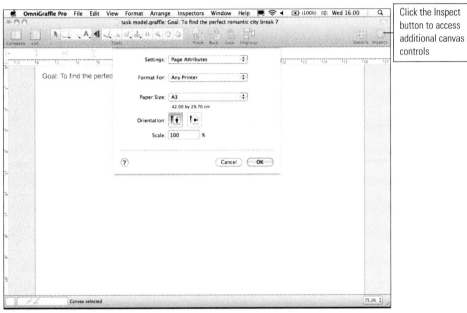

Click the Inspect button to access additional canvas controls

FIGURE 2-13: Using the Page Setup dialog box to choose your canvas size.

Creating the model

With your template now ready, you can begin to add the elements that make up the final task model.

Creating a title for your document

To create a title for your document, simply select the Text Tool button (see Figure 2-14) and then type a title that describes the goal you are representing.

Indicating direction

At its simplest, direction is indicated with a single block arrow through the center of the model (see Figure 2-14). To do this:

1. Open the Stencils window.

2. Select the block arrow and drag it onto your canvas. Move and resize it into the desired position.

3. Select the shape and open the Inspector.

4. Select the Style section to select the Fill color, deselect the Shadow option, and then remove the outline (by un-checking the Stroke box in the Lines and Shapes tab).

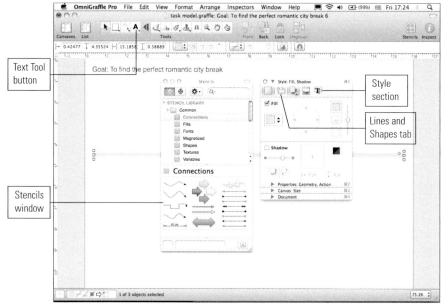

FIGURE 2-14: The title and block arrow are styled and in place. Both the Stencils window and Inspector are open.

Adding individual tasks

To create an individual task, follow these steps:

1 From the Stencil window, select the ellipse and drag it onto the canvas.

2 Resize it making sure it's a perfect circle.

3 Ensure that the fill color is white, remove the shadow and make the outline color the same as the block arrow.

4 Position tasks along the arrow (see Figure 2-15).

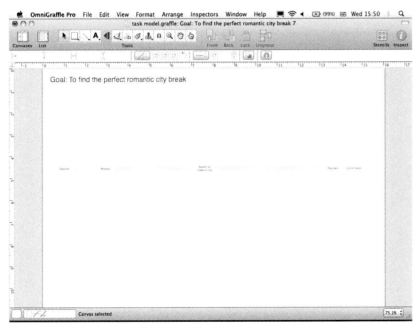

FIGURE 2-15: Individual tasks aligned along the block arrow.

Creating a controlled evaluation

In a controlled evaluation a user should be able to move among all elements in order to make sense of or select a number of different linked components.

The final shape is created by layering a number of individual components on top of each other and styling them appropriately.

❶ Add a circle to the diagram and style it with the same fill color as the block arrow (again removing shadows and outlines). See Figure 2-16.

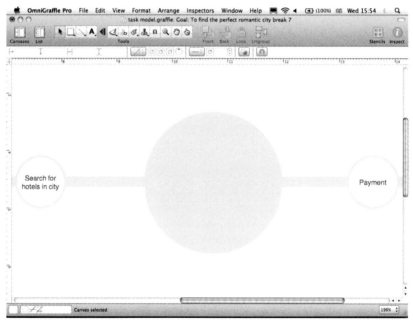

FIGURE 2-16: Adding a circle to the diagram.

❷ Add a second circle on top but this time use the Inspector to give it a white outline. See Figure 2-17.

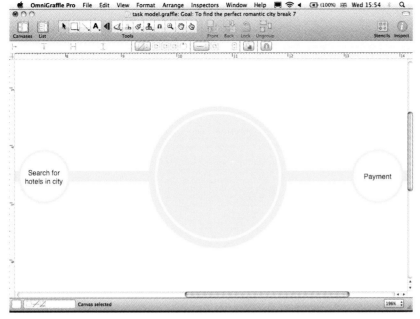

FIGURE 2-17: Adding a second circle with a white outline.

❸ Copy and paste individual tasks (created previously).

❹ Rename the tasks and position the most important task in the center with the remainder around the outside. See Figure 2-18.

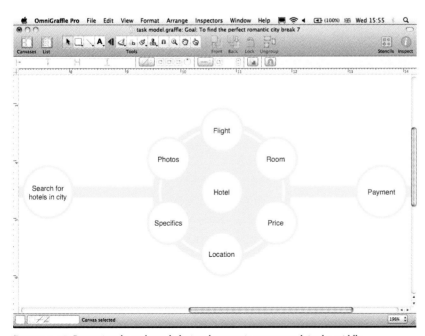

FIGURE 2-18: Renaming the tasks and placing the most important task in the middle.

⑤ Select the line tool from the Toolbar and use connecting lines to join the items together through the center.

⑥ Style the lines to be white. See Figure 2-19.

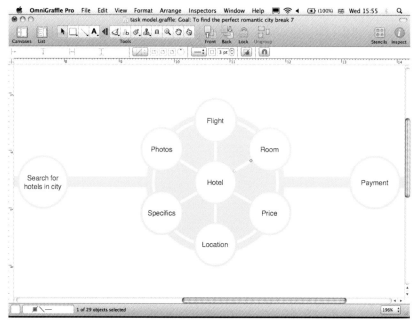

FIGURE 2-19: Using white connecting lines.

tip Make all lines and outlines the same width to help give the diagram a consistent look.

Creating a complex evaluation

Conceptually a complex evaluation is a harder behavior process to understand. Illustrating it is straightforward, however:

① Add a circle to the diagram.

② Copy and paste individual tasks in a random pattern on top of a filled circle.

③ Rename them.

The illusion you want to create is that a user is holding a number of different task considerations in the same state at the same time. See Figure 2-20.

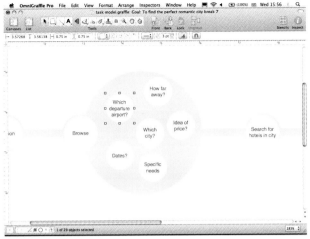

FIGURE 2-20: The complex evaluation. In this example, all the tasks are relating to the core activity of browsing for a holiday.

Creating loop backs

Loop backs are possibly the hardest elements to create. There is no simple way to create smooth arcs with arrowheads in OmniGraffle.

❶ On the Toolbar, click and hold on the Line Tool.

❷ When the options display, select the Bézier curve with the arrowhead.

❸ Add three points on the canvas.

❹ Double-click the last point (this moves you into edit mode rather than continuing to add more points). See Figure 2-21.

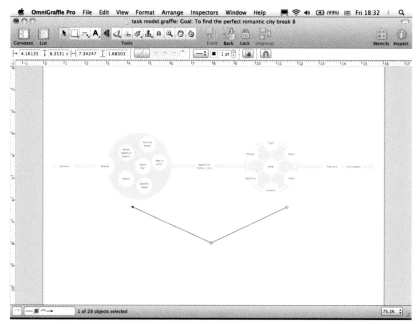

FIGURE 2-21: Adding three points.

⑤ Draw and align two white squares (they will be invisible in the final diagram, but they act as anchor points for the final curve).

⑥ Connect the ends of the arrow to the white squares. See Figure 2-22.

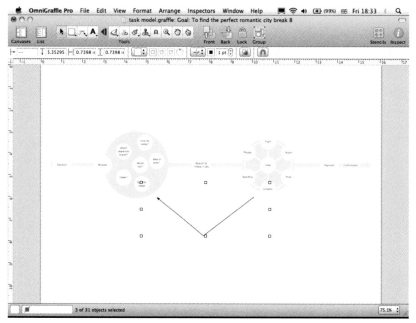

FIGURE 2-22: Connecting the arrows to the squares.

7 Make sure the center point of the line is aligned halfway between the two ends.

8 Holding down the Cmd key, click the center point and pull it out sideways. This reveals the handles, which can then be adjusted to create the curve. See Figure 2-23.

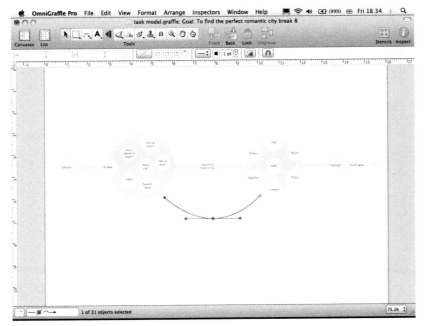

FIGURE 2-23: Curving the line.

9 Finally, style the line by adjusting the stroke width and color. See Figure 2-24.

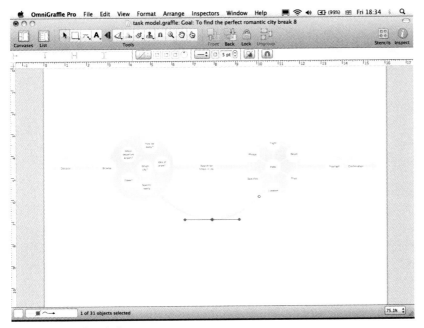

FIGURE 2-24: Styling the line.

Creating notes

To create a note, follow these steps:

1 Select the Line Tool and draw a vertical line between the task model and where you want the note to appear.

2 Select the Text Tool and click and drag on the canvas to create a text box.

3 Add the note.

4 In the Inspector style the text with the desired font and color.

5 Align the text box with the vertical keyline (see Figure 2-25).

If required, barriers and positive elements discussed in notes can be indicated using simple icons (such as the exclamation point shown in Figure 2-25).

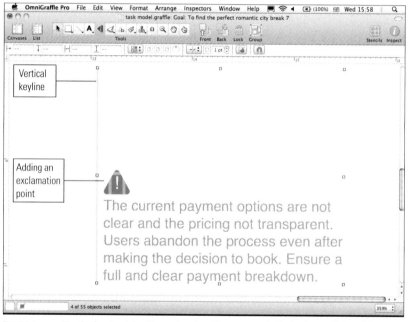

FIGURE 2-25: The final note with callouts showing alignment with the keyline and the addition of an exclamation point.

HOW TO Create task models in PowerPoint

PowerPoint has a solid set of drawing tools that can be used to create sharp-looking task models. PowerPoint is particularly useful when the task model is presented at the same time as findings from a usability test and everything can be created in the same document.

Setting up the template

To set up a template, follow these steps:

❶ Launch PowerPoint, go to the File tab, and select New. A menu of document types displays.

❷ Highlight the Blank presentation then click the Create button on the right.

❸ In the Home tab, in the Slides group, click the Layout button and select the Title Only layout.

You'll find sizing the shapes and aligning the elements much easier if you enable snapping to grid. To do this:

❶ Right-click the slide and choose Grid and Guides.

❷ Select Snap objects to grid (see Figure 2-26).

> **tip** If you want to customize your slide layout we cover this in detail in Chapter 7.

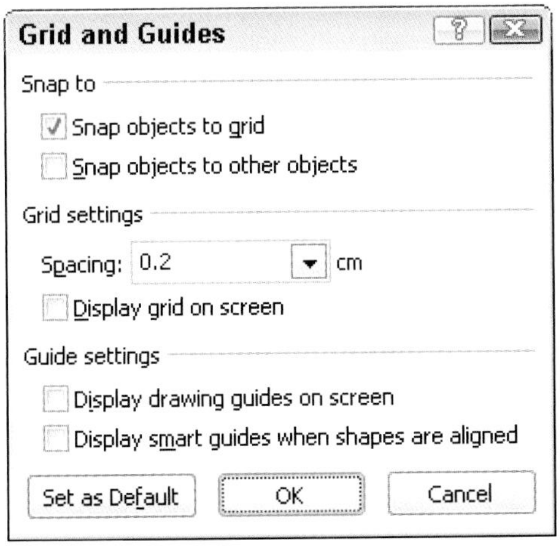

FIGURE 2-26: Selecting the Snap objects to grid option.

Creating the model

Task models are created in PowerPoint by simply styling and aligning shapes. But there are a few tricks that will make getting started easier.

Adding a title

To add a title, follow these steps:

1 Click in the title box and type the goal the task model is illustrating.

2 Resize the title box and reduce the font size to give the task model diagram more room.

Adding the tasks

To add tasks, follow these steps:

1 On the Home tab, in the Drawing group, click the Shapes menu and select the Rounded Rectangle from the shape box. Draw a rectangle on the slide.

2 With the shape selected, in the Drawing group, use the Shape Fill menu to select a pale gray.

3 In the Drawing group, use the Shape Outline menu to select a blue theme color and then change the width.

4 Type the task name and then style the text using the font controls in the Home tab.

tip Right-clicking any shape allows you to select the Format Shape dialog, which allows you to control the style of the shape from a single location.

5 Copy and paste the original task for each of the remaining tasks and rename them.

note Depending on the number of tasks, it might be necessary to resize the rectangles and type size to allow the tasks to fit into the same slide.

Occasionally, you might need to enlarge slide area in the page set-up (this helps the layout, and you can scale it back down to a side of A4 you print).

6 Align the shapes—this is where snapping to grid comes into its own.

⑦ In the Drawing group, click the Shapes menu and choose connecting lines. Draw lines between the individual tasks. These are magnetized to allow them to snap to the edge of other shapes.

tip Use arrows only where necessary to indicate the direction of the task. Using arrows everywhere can clutter the diagram.

⑧ In the Drawing group, use the Shape Outline menu to style the connecting lines and arrows using the same color and thickness as the outline of the rounded rectangle. This helps join the elements together visually. See Figure 2-27.

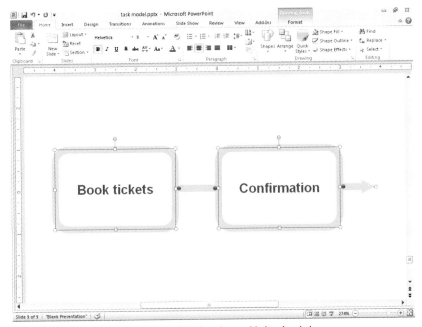

FIGURE 2-27: The tasks and connecting lines have been added and styled.

Creating a controlled evaluation

The simplest way to create a controlled evaluation is to build it from a series of shapes layered on top of each other. As with creating tasks, use the shape menu to select the shape and then style them using the fill and outline controls.

1 Draw a filled circle for the background (see Figure 2-28).

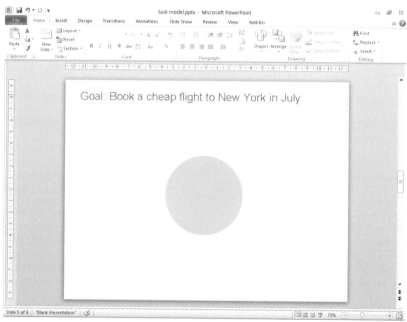

FIGURE 2-28: Drawing the circle.

2 Layer a circle with a pale outline (and no fill) over the top to form the connection lines between the task boxes (see Figure 2-29).

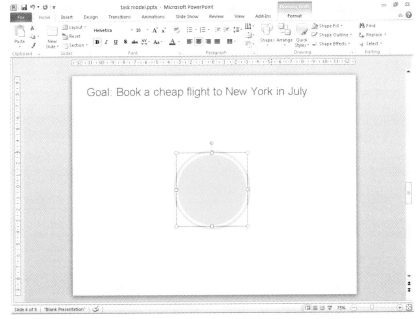

FIGURE 2-29: Layering the circle.

❸ Position the task blocks around the edge of the circle (see Figure 2-30).

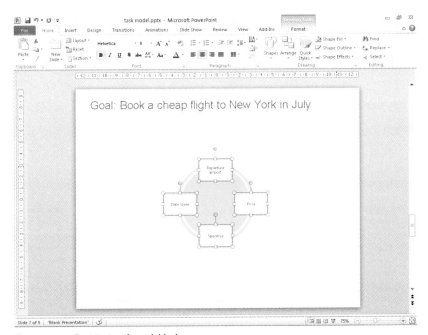

FIGURE 2-30: Positioning the task blocks.

❹ Use connecting lines to join the opposite shapes (see Figure 2-31).

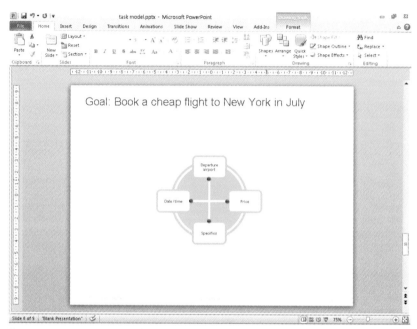

FIGURE 2-31: Using connecting lines to join the shapes.

Creating simple icons

You can easily create icons that help illustrate your task model by combining a few shapes. Again, shapes are selected from the Shapes menu and styled accordingly. Figure 2-32 shows how two circles and a rectangle have been grouped together and resized to create a simple person icon.

Standard shapes within PowerPoint can also be adapted to illustrate a point. Figure 2-33 shows a rounded block arrow that has been styled to indicate an iterative process.

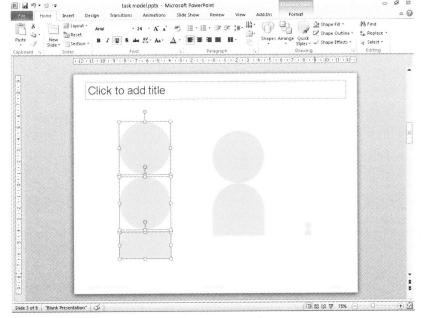

FIGURE 2-32: Two circles and a rectangle have been grouped to create a person icon.

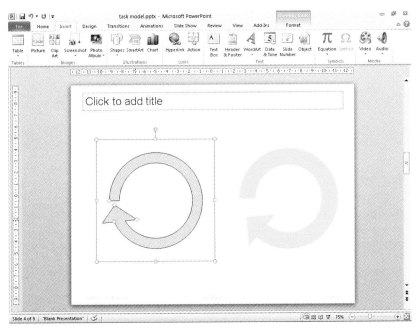

FIGURE 2-33: Standard shapes can be selected and styled to create simple icons.

Adding the finishing touches

From the Shapes menu, select text boxes and lines to add the notes relating to the task model.

Information from one of the project's personas and user quotes are added to give color to the persona and make it real for the project team. The persona photo is added by clicking the Insert tab and then clicking the Picture button.

tip Black and white photos often work better because they are less distracting than color photos.

Figure 2-34 shows the completed task model.

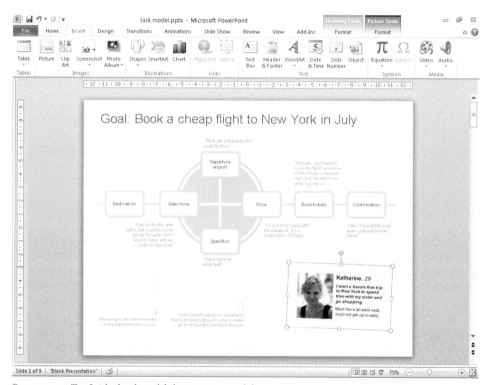

FIGURE 2-34: The finished task model showing notes and the persona summary.

Chapter 3

User Journeys

3

USER JOURNEYS DETAIL the exact steps a user goes through to complete a task or goal. They differ from task models in that they show the required interactions and paths through a system rather than being a representation of desired user behavior. They also differ from sitemaps as they show specific routes through a site rather than the logical structure of the entire site. However, the three documents need to align with each other and you will find yourself working back and forth between them ensuring that the desired user experience matches.

This chapter focuses on detailed, system-based user journeys (see Figure 3-1) rather than the broad journeys a user might take as he moves between online and offline activities.

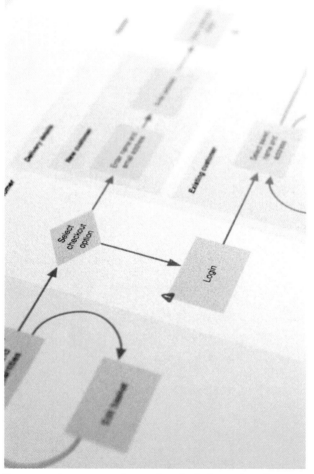

FIGURE 3-1: A user journey showing the individual steps through a system to complete a task.

What makes a good user journey?

A good user journey reflects the behavior uncovered in the task model, which is developed through research and observation. Ensuring that the task model and user journey match is an important way of checking that the system you are creating meets the needs of the user.

A user journey is a great document to help you figure out how elements of a site will flow together and is helpful when discussing the options with the team. User journeys are easy to sketch out on a whiteboard or by using Post-it Notes. You can map out the wireframes against them, ensuring that the right content elements are on each page.

When to create a user journey

There are two scenarios where user journeys should always be created:

> **Product development.** Create a user journey when developing a system from scratch. For example, you're working with a client to develop a new check-out process and you need to understand the best way to implement it.

> **Analysis.** Create a user journey when testing has shown that the current user journey is broken and needs to be fixed. For example, when an confusing check-out process journey can be redesigned to increase conversion.

Product development

User journeys should be created when you are developing a new product or service. They help you understand the system that the user requires to be built and help make sure that you can match it in the interface (for example, do you have the right links to the right places on each page?) and with the technical implementation (for example, can the right data calls be made at the required points?).

Develop the user journey once you have a solid set of personas and task models to base it on; these will both inform it and help you check that you have the right user journey. Conducting benchmark testing of an existing service (for example, testing on a previous version of the product or on a competitor's products) will help to identify problems with the user journey that need fixing and help you avoid the same mistakes.

To help ensure that the user journey is optimized—and only if time allows for this—explore more than one user journey and test each both during development and once the product is launched. This can be helpful for processes such as an e-commerce checkout where you can test the performance of asking for all customer details on one page versus splitting them over a number of pages. Both solutions are usable, but the real-world performance and conversion might vary.

Analysis

User journeys are excellent documents to produce after user testing or after expert reviews have been carried out on an existing product or service. They enable you to step back from the page-by-page analysis to view the journey as a whole. This can be done a number of ways:

> You can show the existing user journey and describe the positives and pain points (see Figure 3-2).

> You can show how the existing user journey needs to be adapted to better serve the needs of the user.

> You can revise the user journey completely based on the needs of the user.

> Or you can show how the existing journey can be expanded with newly uncovered journeys.

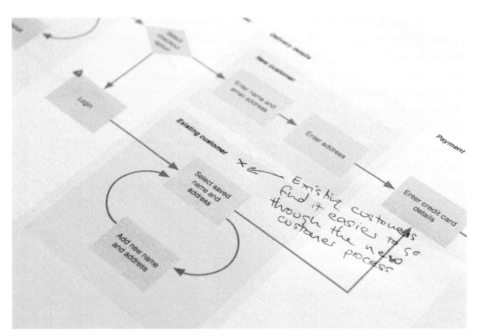

FIGURE 3-2: Analyzing a user journey can show you pain points and where the journey can be refined.

What are you communicating?

The following elements can typically be illustrated in a user journey.

The goal or task

Use the goal or task as the page title. This is the user desired outcome from the journey. For example, this might be the user's desire to buy the items in the shopping cart.

Steps

In a user journey diagram a single block represents a specific step users must do to complete their journey. This could be a piece of information for them to review or an item of data that they need to submit. For example, it might be their need to enter their mailing address or their credit card information.

Decision points

Decision points are used when a user has to make a choice in order to carry on through the journey—picking a car color out of a range of available colors, for example. The result could be to go on to a single next step with that selection made, or for two or more resultant branches in the user journey diagram showing alternate routes.

Start and end steps

Start and end steps illustrate the beginning and the end of the user journey. Using different shaped blocks helps these to stand out. For example, the start of the journey might illustrate the addition of items to the basket and the end of the journey might confirm that the products have been purchased.

Grouping

A single step can be on a page of its own. If there are several steps on a single page, grouping needs to be shown. This could be where the name, address and contact information is grouped together on a personal details page.

Flow

Single and double-headed arrows can be used to show the direction in which the user can move between tasks or steps. Using curved arrows back to a previous step can be a more effective way of illustrating where users are repeating the same task (or tasks) one or more times. Editing a cart on an online store is a good example of an iterative process.

Content

It can be useful to add any content requirements onto the user journey without which the journey could not be completed. For example, you might find that users require a summary of the products they are buying to be carried through each step of the checkout to reassure them that everything they want is indeed being purchased. These should also be added to the content requirements document.

Pain points

In conducting analysis on an existing user journey, a clear illustration of pain points helps the project team to focus on the elements that need to be fixed.

External factors

Are there elements a user needs to complete the task that are outside of the system on which you are focusing? This could be external sites, conversations, and so on. It's important to show the interrelationships to build as accurate a user journey as possible.

Measurement

If your user journey is of an existing system, analytics can be overlaid onto the diagram to show the actual usage of specific elements. If you are creating a user journey for a new system, then it is a good idea to include the measurement points so you can track how users interact with the system to help with the ongoing analysis and improvement.

The anatomy of a user journey

User journeys are functional documents. Styling is kept to a minimum in order to let the design and development team focus on the flow and detail of the content. See Figure 3-3.

Title

The title is a simple summary of the goal the user needs to achieve.

Groupings

Groupings are the pages or phases that the steps group into. In this example, they're nested to show a split in the journey for different user groups. Shading shows how elements are nested together.

Start steps and end steps

Start steps and end steps are the elements that trigger the step and the last things that happen. Depending on your project it might be necessary to show how several user journeys join together. These are indicated through simply rounding the corners.

Steps

A step is the action that needs to be performed by the user or the content that he needs to review.

Pain points

Pain points from existing research can be added to individual steps to show where something needs refining.

Decision points

Decision points illustrate the steps that cause a split in the user journey. A diamond is used.

Flow

The flow is simply the direction a user can move in between steps. It's shown by one- or two-way arrows and iterative loops.

Notes

Notes are spaces to record key learning and communication points.

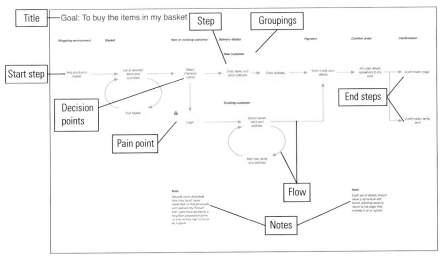

FIGURE 3-3: An example user journey showing the key elements to include.

Who is the audience?

Like most user experience documentation, the user journey's audience spans the different roles on the project team. At a high level, the whole team will need to understand the flow and associated freedom (or restriction) of movement you've uncovered through user research and documented in the task model. At a detailed level, the user journey uncovers exactly what needs to happen at each stage as a user moves through a site—and therefore where the content and data need to sit to support it.

I've divided the audience according to their different practical needs:

> **Business analysts and project managers.** They care about the detail of the user journey. They will want to make sure that all required elements have been accounted for and that the process can be developed as specified on time and budget.

> **The development team.** They want to make sure that the development and framework they are using can support the journey specified. For example, if an off-the-shelf e-commerce package is being used, how can it be adapted to match the required user journey?

> **Copywriters, designers,** and the **wireframe team.** They need to understand the overall flow of the user journey. It will help to identify the number of pages and templates needed and beyond that help them consider how to create consistency in style and interaction as a user moves between the pages.

> **Business stakeholders.** Does the user journey meet the practical, functional and monetary business needs? Will users be able to easily complete the tasks and have a positive experience?

How to validate the user journey

When you've completed research to set up the user journey (see the research and workshop ideas later in this chapter), you'll have a lot of confidence that the journey you're creating is the right one. You can validate and optimize the user journey at several times during the development process, first on prototypes and later on the live site.

User testing of wireframes, designs, and live sites

Testing sites, applications, and their prototypes frequently expose problems that relate to the user journey (and often task model).

If you see that the process isn't meeting user expectations (if users don't know what's coming next, or that they can't do things or find information at the right time), then you'll need to step back and revise the user journey.

If you've completed a full user-centered design process, you're less likely to find that this is the case than if you've jumped straight into user testing toward the end of a project.

A/B testing and multivariate testing (MVT)

A/B and multivariate testing allow you to test the real-world performance of two or more design variables against each other to uncover which combination of variables is most effective for the completion of tasks (see Figure 3-4). A/B testing typically looks at two variables; MVT allows for many more variations.

Before completing A/B or MVT testing, ensure that all candidate solutions are usable (by developing them as part of a user-centered design process) so you have the confidence that none of the solutions will break the site.

You can test the user journey at three levels:

> Element level to test that specific form fields and pieces of content are in the right place and executed in the best way.

> Group level to test the order of chunks of content on a page.

> Page level to test the optimal flow through the site.

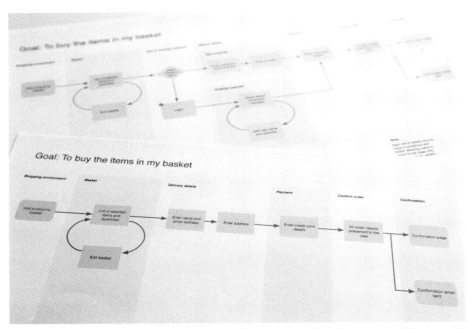

FIGURE 3-4: A/B testing and MVT testing can help you decide which variables of a user journey (all proven to be usable) will perform better for the business.

RESEARCH AND WORKSHOP IDEAS

Researching and defining user journeys is always fun and enlightening. You begin to take the learning's from the persona and task model development and use them to create the actual experience users will have on the site.

In research, participants feel like they are helping to shape the site around their needs and engage well. In workshops, the project team can work together to discuss and debate the ideal user journeys.

RESEARCH TECHNIQUE: Process sorting

In process sorting, you use the same materials as when using card sorting, using labels on cards, or when using Post-it Notes (see Figure 3-5), but you get participants to put the cards in the order they expect or want things to happen. If relevant, have the participants group the cards into items they think will appear on the same page.

FIGURE 3-5: A participant uses Post-it Notes to show how she expects a journey to work.

Note any problems the users have with terminology and create new cards where participants require additional steps (they might also not want all the steps that the organization wants).

Remember that users might have different user journeys depending on what they are trying to complete, so try a number of different tasks with the same participant to see how the user journey might need to be adapted in each instance. For example, on a travel site, you want to understand the user journey for booking a flight and a user journey for booking both a flight with a hotel. You'll see where each journey overlaps and where the differences that need to be accommodated are. This is helpful because you're ultimately trying to understand how to fit all the required elements together in order to create the best experience for the user.

Once you've established the basic journey that the participant is after, use the cards to explore the next more granular level of information and understand the content and data requirements at each stage. Ask open and non-leading questions such as "What information would you expect to complete here?" and "What information do you need to be able to do that?" Matching a system to the user expectations of how it should work makes the completed product immensely more satisfying for the user. For example, knowing that you'll make your customers happy by just asking for their names and email addresses on a sign-up page is far better than asking them to also provide their dates of birth and mobile numbers—which they are not happy to submit. Another example is to provide a clothing size guide next to where customers select the sizes of garments—it gives them the information they need, when they want it.

You'll end up with a number of processes (one for each participant) that you can analyze and uncover common patterns. Behind each step you'll also have a note of user content requirements, which you can feed into the content audit documentation.

This analysis and research forms the basis of your user journey document.

WORKSHOP IDEA: Examine user journeys

A user journey workshop with the project team is a good way to map out and discuss all elements of a user journey. Before you begin, you should have completed your research using the process-sorting technique described at the beginning of this section. This ensures you can play the role of the users (championing what they want—not what you or the project team thinks).

Inviting attendees

Invite a wide range of project stakeholders including designers, developers, business analysts, project managers, product managers, and marketers.

Ask the participants to prepare and bring information on their area of expertise—whether it's the content requirements, data requirements, or information on the technical platform—and any existing analytics. Aside from the user insights, this information helps ensure that you have the right level of detail to make informed decisions about how the journey should look.

Gathering materials

Try to use a room with a whiteboard so that Post-it Notes can easily be stuck up and moved and that lines connecting the elements can be drawn or rubbed out. Have a camera on hand so that you can document the user journey in different states as it evolves (you might need to roll back to a previous version either during the meeting or later in the project process).

Also have on hand the personas and task model so that user goals and behavior are reflected in the journey.

Conducting the Workshop

To conduct the workshop, follow these steps:

1. Start at a high level and get the attendees to share the phases and groupings (such as delivery details or billing information) that need to be in the user journey. Don't worry about the detail just yet.

2. Match the groups against the user requirements and functional requirements, discussing where the two clash (for example, cite differences between the information a user wants to input against the information a company wants to collect).

3. Put the groups in order and think about the flow between them. Are users able to move in one or two directions between elements or can they apply filters that allow them to iteratively refine a list?

This gives you your basic user journey and while it seems straightforward, experience has shown that it will generate a lot of detailed discussions around how the system (or an element of a system) is put together.

4. Work through the individual data and content requirements that are needed to support each step of the journey. Again, you can use the functional and user requirements to ensure that the detail is covered.

> **tip** Use different colored Post-it Notes to differentiate the content requirements from the steps they belong to.

If you're creating a user journey from scratch, use the user journey workshop (see Figure 3-6) as an opportunity to identify the different measurement points necessary to understanding user behavior and assessing the success of the project.

FIGURE 3-6: In a user journey workshop, collaborate with the project team to create the user journey.

What's the simplest way to illustrate the user journey?

HOW TO Create a user journey in OmniGraffle

There are lots of similarities between creating sitemaps, task models, and user journeys in OmniGraffle. Depending on the result you are trying to achieve, you might want to cross-reference those chapters.

Setting up the template

The following steps show you how to resize the canvas and set up a grid structure. This simplifies the process of creating the user journey.

❶ Launch OmniGraffle. The default templates are displayed. Select the blank template and click the New Diagram button.

❷ Change the canvas size to A3 (420mm by 297mm). This setting provides a large canvas area to work on and scales down nicely to US Letter or A4.

❸ Click File and choose Page Set-up.

❹ In the Paper Size drop-down, choose the Manage Custom Sizes option.

❺ Click the + icon, give your paper size a name (in this case, A3), and type the dimensions 420 mm by 297 mm.

Next, you need to set up a grid structure for the document. The following steps create graph paper-style markings on the canvas area and allow you to control the sizing, spacing, and alignment of shapes with precision. Figure 3-7 illustrates how the finished selections will look.

❶ In the toolbar, click the Inspect button to open the Inspect window.

❷ In the Canvas: Grid tab, click the Ruler Units button and change the unit of measurement to centimeters.

❸ Click the Grid button and in the Major Grid Spacing text field, type 1cm (see Figure 3-7).

❹ Change the Minor Grid Steps to 4 (equivalent to 2.5mm).

❺ In the same panel, select the Snap to grid option.

❻ Select the Show grid lines checkbox and the Show major checkbox.

❼ The Edges on grid radio button should be selected by default. If not, select it. This ensures the edges (rather than centers of objects) align to the grid.

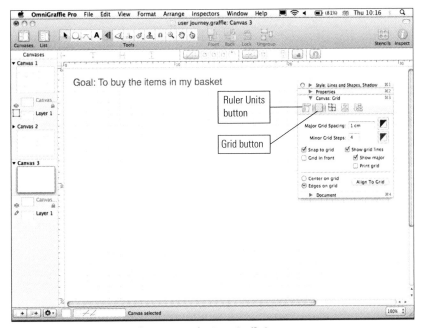

FIGURE 3-7: Setting up the grid structure in the OmniGraffle Inspector.

Creating the journey

The following guide gives you all the information you need to create the journey. While the result looks simple, there is an art to laying out the elements into an easy to read document.

Providing a title

To provide a title, follow these steps:

❶ From the toolbar, select the Text Tool.

❷ Place the cursor where you want to the title to appear on the canvas and title your user journey with the goal or task you are representing.

note Refer to Figure 2-14 in Chapter 2 for an overview of OmniGraffle's text controls.

Styling shapes

The Stencil Library has useful default shapes that can be used to create attractive user journeys. Figure 3-8 shows the Stencil window and style controls.

❶ On the Toolbar, click the Stencils button to open the Stencils window.

❷ In the Stencils library, open the Software folder and click the Flow Chart stencil.

❸ Select the Flow Chart shapes you need and drag them onto the canvas. The most commonly used shapes are the Start/Stop, Process, and Decision shapes.

❹ The default shapes can be styled in the Style window to create the master elements:

- Turn off Shadow and Stroke as they add unnecessary visual clutter to the document.

- Select a Fill color and Font color with good contrast to ensure legibility both on screen and when printed.

❺ Copy and paste the styled shapes as many times as needed and position them to create the outline user journey.

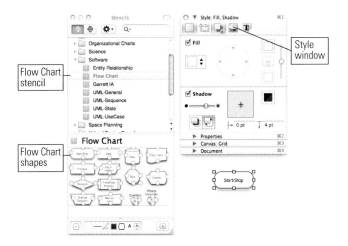

FIGURE 3-8: An overview of OmniGraffle's Stencil window and Style window.

Using magnetic shapes and arrows

Using magnets means that when you move shapes, the arrows move with them and that saves time when you're rearranging the layout. OmniGraffle gives you good control over the magnetic properties of objects.

❶ Select a shape.

❷ Open the Inspect palette, open the Properties section, and then click the Connections button (see Figure 3-9).

❸ In the Shapes, Groups and Tables section, check Allow connections from lines (if it isn't already selected). This makes your shape magnetic.

❹ In the 4 magnets drop down, you can select where you want the magnets to be on your shape. Typically you'll just need N, S, E, W selected, but you can also choose the corners and number of magnets per side.

Now when you add connecting lines, they will snap to the magnets added to your shapes.

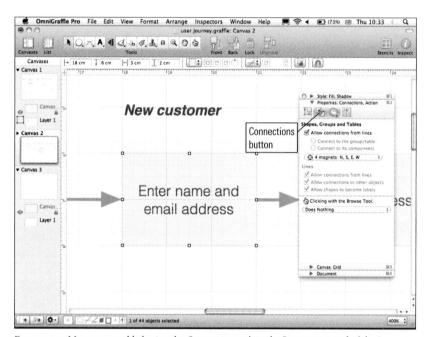

FIGURE 3-9: Magnets are added using the Connections tab in the Properties panel of the Inspector.

Adding lines and arrows

To add lines and arrows, follow these steps:

❶ In the Toolbar, click the Line Tool (see Figure 3-10) and then select the line type you want to use to connect your shapes. We use Straight and Orthogonal.

❷ Draw lines between your shapes connecting the line ends to the magnets.

❸ Style your lines using the Style: Lines and Shapes, Shadow inspector.

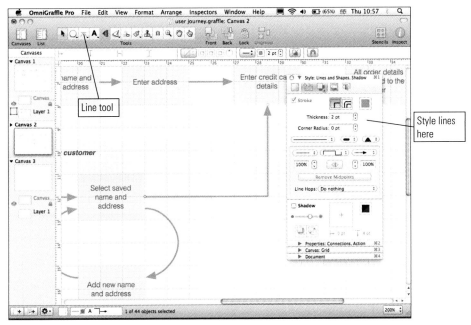

FIGURE 3-10: Adding and styling lines in OmniGraffle.

Styling the curved arrows

To style curved arrows, follow these steps:

❶ In the Toolbar, click the Line Tool and then select the Bézier line.

❷ Add three points to the canvas equally around an imaginary center point.

❸ Connect the two end points to the magnetized shapes.

❹ Click the center point and move the position of the handles until you have created a semi-circle. Figure 3-11 shows how the handles are positioned.

note To create a quarter circle, use the same technique only add just two points and move the handles of each.

COMMUNICATING THE USER EXPERIENCE

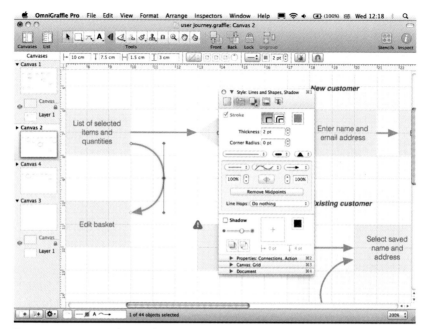

FIGURE 3-11: A semi-circle created using a Bézier curve showing the handle positions.

Finishing off

Where steps are grouped into pages in the example, zebra stripes are used in the background to mark out the individual pages. These are simply lightly shaded rectangles sent to the back of the other items. On occasion you'll have to show two options within the same page (for example, how new customers and existing customers are handled at the same point in a journey); a shade between the zebra stripes and the individual steps is used to nest these items together. See Figure 3-12.

tip As you're working on documents such as user journeys and sitemaps, the alignment can go slightly off. In the Inspect palette (where you set up the grids), there is a button titled Align to grid. Clicking this button resizes shapes and aligns objects back to the grid, saving you a lot of hassle doing it all manually.

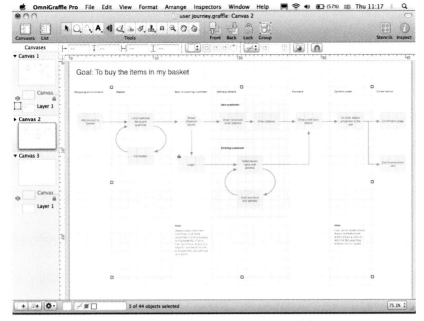

FIGURE 3-12: Shaded rectangles illustrate the pages in the journey and the grouping of steps.

HOW TO Create a user journey in PowerPoint

Creating user journeys in PowerPoint is really straightforward but there are a few tricks to creating a good-looking diagram.

Setting up the template

The user journey template is set up in the same way you set up template for task models in Chapter 2:

❶ Launch PowerPoint, go to the File tab, and select New. A menu of document types is shown.

❷ Click the Blank presentation then click the Create button on the right.

❸ On the Home tab, click on the Layout button and choose the Title Slide layout.

You'll find sizing the shapes and aligning the elements much easier if you enable snapping to grid:

❶ Right-click the slide area and choose Grid and Guides.

❷ Select Snap objects to grid (see Figure 3-13).

❸ You should also enable the Display grid on screen option. This provides you with a series of guide dots that helps alignment, but does increase the visual clutter as you're working on the document.

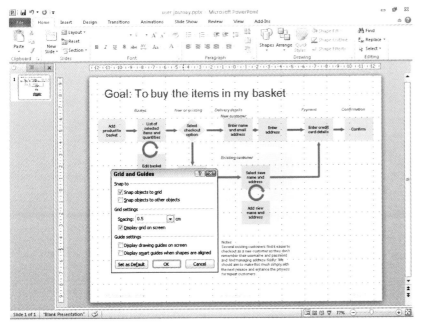

FIGURE 3-13: The Grid and Guides dialog with the Snap objects to grid option enabled and the Display grid on screen option enabled.

Depending on the size of your user journey, you might need to give yourself a larger slide area to work on. To do this, click on the Design tab and select Page Setup in the top left. Here you can choose a number of ratios and dimensions. There's usually a little trial and error to get everything scaled and fitting neatly on a single slide — of course you can always divide the document over multiple slides to be printed out and stuck together on walls.

Creating the journey

The journey is simply a series of aligned shapes.

Adding shapes

To add shapes, follow these steps:

1 Click the Home tab and in the Drawing group, click the Shapes menu and choose your shape.

2 Style your shapes using the Shape Fill and Shape Outline buttons.

Changing shapes

Once you've created and styled a shape, you can copy and paste the shape by using the Edit menu. You can then use the Change Shape option (see Figure 3-14) and retain the styling of the original shape:

1 Select the shape.

2 Click the Format tab.

3 Click the Edit Shape button.

4 Choose Change Shape.

5 Select the shape that you want to use.

User journeys primarily use rectangles, rounded rectangles, or diamonds to illustrate the steps, start points, end points, and decisions.

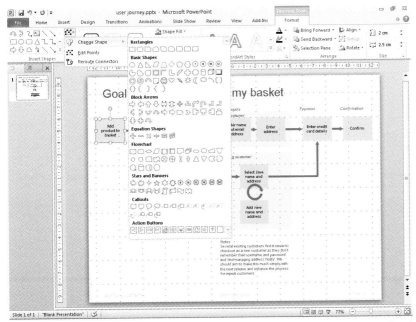

FIGURE 3-14: Use the Change Shape menu to copy and paste a shape and change it into another shape while keeping the original styling.

Wrapping text

Diamond shapes allow for only a limited amount of text inside them. To control where the line breaks appear and to get the text fitting nicely, you'll need to complete the following steps:

1. Right-click the shape and click Format shape.

2. In the window that displays, select Text Box from the left menu.

3. Deselect the Wrap text option.

4. To control where you want the line breaks to appear, place the cursor in the desired position and enter a soft line break (press Shift+Enter).

Adding arrows and lines

Use Arrows and Elbow Arrow Connectors to join the shapes together. Use Circular Arrows to indicate the steps users can repeat several times. Follow these steps:

1 In the Drawing group, click the Shapes menu and choose the desired connector lines and arrows.

2 Draw them between the shapes and connect them to the anchor points.

3 Adjust the outline and fill colors so that the shapes and lines look good on screen and have enough contrast to print out well.

Finishing up

Grouped steps are indicated by placing shaded rectangles in the background. These can be nested where more than one grouping needs to be shown.

Figure 3-15 shows the completed user journey.

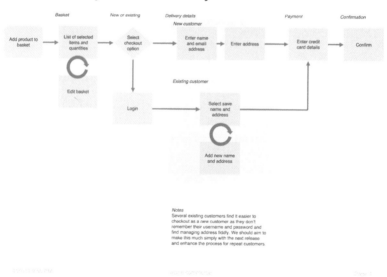

FIGURE 3-15: The finished user journey in PowerPoint showing the edited colors.

Chapter

Content Requirements

EVERY PROJECT WE'VE worked on and every piece of research we've conducted touches on the text and images that need to be presented to the user. It's probably surprising then that most content documents don't focus on or even mention the user needs.

This chapter shows how to put together a simple document to collect content requirements (see Figure 4-1) from users in a consistent way throughout the project.

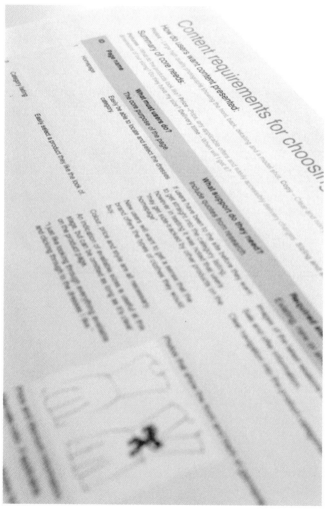

FIGURE 4-1: A contents requirement document.

What makes a good content requirements document?

A great content requirements document focuses on the user needs—specifically what content (text, image, sound, and video) needs to be provided to enable a user to fulfill a goal.

When to create a content requirements document?

Content requirements start to be uncovered very early, long before you know how the final product will work or look. So it's worth discussing and setting up a template to capture the requirements at the beginning of the project.

The result is a consistent template to capture content needs as they emerge from workshops with stakeholders and research with users. Rather than having to work from several documents (for example, task models, personas, and user test reports—although these should contain requirements uncovered in those phases of work), you have one consistent checklist that ensures all the required information is communicated in the final product and in the right way.

What are you communicating?

By understanding the different types of content, you develop a framework for talking through the requirements with the project team (it's often the case that different people are responsible for different types of content, such as copy or photography). And when it comes to wireframing and designing, understanding the content requirements can help establish the design patterns and styles that are needed throughout the interface.

Marketing and brand copy

Marketing and brand copy sets the purpose of the page through the title and description. The tone and style will be set by the business and can be tested with users to ensure clarity and appropriateness.

Within the main content of the page, the brand provides an emotional reason to engage with a product or service. This can come through expectations of the brand through prior knowledge or by allowing users to decide that the brand is one that they can have an affinity with and reinforces their beliefs. Some examples of marketing and brand content could be:

> How products are made

> How a bank invests its money

> An organization's charitable activities

Users care about this information. If it's not there, they will notice. And they might use another product or service instead.

Instructions and functionality

The functional content defines exactly what users must do in order to get to the next step of their goals. For example, on a product site, a customer might need to select the quantity and size of items before adding them to her shopping cart. The wording needs to be clear and the action must be obvious.

Data and specification information

What data do users need in order to make a decision? This could be straightforward, such as the price of the product, or it might be an element that's very specific such as needing the trunk capacity of an automobile (everybody has niggling requirements that need to be satisfied). These specific requirements are always uncovered through user research.

Image requirements

Photography is the unsung hero of user experience. Users want to see large, good quality photos that satisfy their specific needs or curiosity. This is particularly true when decisions have to be made, whether it's a product purchase, the choice of where to go on vacation, or which company to work for.

You frequently see photos in user testing where brands have applied a house style or cropped images to make them artistic or in keeping with the design when in fact users just want to see the product in as much detail and in as large a size as possible.

Sometimes the right photos aren't provided, so they can't help the user make a decision. Product choices are the obvious example. If you are choosing a dress, you want to know exactly what both the front and back look like before you buy it—if you can't see the back of the dress, you won't buy it. But it is also true for more information rich sites. Universities and college sites need to let prospective students know what the campus is like, information about the town and city where it's situated, and what the other students will be like. Dated or low-quality photography will present a poor impression.

Supporting information

Research uncovers the supplementary information a user requires to support and reassure her that she's making the right decision. Taking an e-commerce example again, this could be the delivery and returns information, information about the cut of a garment, or information about the material it's made from. Offering the product without this supporting information will leave the user with doubts as to whether this is the right purchase for her.

What makes the perfect content requirements document?

Perfect content requirements ensure that you communicate user information requirements to the project team effectively.

The sample document shown in Figure 4-2 is goal based—what users need in order to buy a boutique dress. It helps communicate the requirements more effectively and maps more easily onto the task models and user journeys. When you develop your sitemap and wireframes, it is used as a checklist to make sure everything is accounted for on each section and page.

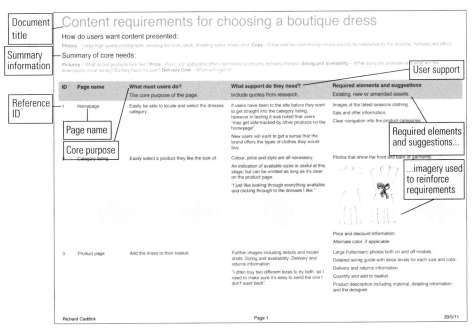

FIGURE 4-2: The perfect content requirements document showing the required information.

Document title

The document title gives the goal of the user covered in the requirements document.

Summary information

Content requirements documents can get very large. Summary information—pulling out the key themes and presentation information—is a useful way of summarizing the requirements to the project team.

Reference ID

A unique reference ID helps you to pinpoint rows as you're discussing them with the project team and allows you to cross-reference the document easily.

Page name

The page name references the page or section of the site is being referred to. Under most circumstances, there will be multiple content requirements for one page. For a new site, this might not be known exactly until after the sitemap is developed, but a reference to the step in the task will work well.

Core purpose

What must users do? This is the core purpose of the page—the one or two things users must do in order to continue their journeys.

User support

What content do users need in order to make the decision to continue their journeys? This type of user support could be a combination of functional, data, imagery, information, or brand. Figure 4-2 shows how you can include quotes from users to add grounded reality into content discussions.

Required elements and suggestions

Very often in the user-centered design process, you'll identify pieces of content and images that do exactly what a user requires. Required elements and suggestions could be from an existing site, competitor sites, or other relevant information. You might also sketch out suggestions and write example content to better illustrate the requirements to the project team, not to be used as final assets, but to help facilitate meaningful discussion. Figure 4-2 shows how imagery has been included to reinforce the requirement.

Additional columns can be added depending on the specific needs of the project and this document could be expanded into a more complete content matrix, which might also include the URL of the page, who is responsible for the content, and what the process is for getting it produced. These tasks can fall outside of the user experience role so an expanded document would need to be worked on with the relevant parts of the project team.

Who is the audience?

The content requirements touch every part of a business because they range from how a product or service is presented to users down to what data needs to be stored and presented to the user.

In particular, the content and copy team will be able to take the user requirements and develop the words that clearly communicate the messages and brand voice. The project managers and business analysts will want to ensure that the content can be sourced and accommodated for as part of the development. And the user experience team will be responsible for making sure all the requirements are fed into the sitemaps and wireframes.

Of course, the reality is that not all the content needs can be fulfilled in the short term, so the requirements document will help to shape future content strategy.

Validating the content

If the right content isn't presented to users at the right time and in the right way they will struggle to reach their goals. Validating that the right content is in place will make a huge difference to the success of the project.

Content testing in context

As you're testing wireframes and designs, you are implicitly testing the content that is presented. Using the think-aloud protocol (encouraging users to think out loud as they are completing a task on a website) will help you assess whether users' questions and expectations are being met, allowing them to do what they need to. Be sure to explore how people feel about the images and information and assess whether the right data and functions are available to them. Finally, see if there is anything about the tone that they are particularly attracted to or find off-putting.

tip Testing little and often over the course of a project is recommended. Testing with five users at five times during the project will ensure that the project is more successful than testing with 25 users at the end.

Frequently the first user testing completed uncovers the big problems and omissions. Then as you address those problems over the course of the project, the testing starts to validate the decisions you've made giving confidence in a successful product when it goes live. It's important to get a new set of participants each time you test to ensure that you've properly solved the problems and that the users aren't just learning how to use a faulty process.

Content variation testing

Sometimes it can be helpful to take the content out of context, focusing in on a participant's response to different executions of the same copy or alternate photographic treatments.

Here's an outline of a frequently used approach. Take a key wireframe from the user journey (a product page on an e-commerce site in this example) and try two or three versions using different executions of the same content—for example, different treatments of the imagery (see Figure 4-3) or different wording for the headlines.

FIGURE 4-3: The same wireframe is tested with two different leading images to see which performs better in research and why.

Conduct research with users to understand which variations of content best support their needs the best and, perhaps more importantly, don't create barriers for them when they're completing tasks. Participants are very good at pointing out changes that the project team misses.

This testing not only improves the quality of the content, it uncovers the stories and reasons behind the likes and dislikes that help enrich the understanding of user behavior and therefore the personas and task models you produce.

RESEARCH AND WORKSHOP IDEAS

Coming to grips with content is immensely satisfying. It's the raw material that a product or service is built on and yet it is often deprioritized in processes behind wireframes, design, and build.

RESEARCH TECHNIQUE: Immerse yourself in the topic

Every time you start working on a new project, immerse yourself in the subject matter.

Buy the relevant journals and magazines, look at the sites and user forums, and start to understand the trends, passions, frustrations, questions, and solutions that people are talking about and that are being presented to them.

If possible, find places where you can observe people in the real world, whether it's at the shopping mall, in an office, at a store (see Figure 4-4), or elsewhere.

All these activities help you to get closer to people and allow you to have better empathy for the lives they lead.

FIGURE 4-4: Take photos to remind you what people did so you can recall better stories. In this case, the picture might remind you how the customer chose between the various products in front of her.

WORKSHOP IDEA: Audit content

At the beginning of the project take time to audit any existing content with the project team. Assess what people like and don't like and the areas for improvement.

Before the workshop, ask the attendees to collate examples of content they like. This could be from competitor sites, sites they like, magazines, or newspapers. Get them to share their ideas in turn and listen to their reasoning.

Then work at a broad level through the project you are involved with, discussing the effectiveness of headings, imagery, and informational and data-driven content. Understand whether it meets the needs of the organization and what is missing that needs communicating. Match it against examples the team collated to see how it could be enriched or changed.

Print out, draw, or write example assets onto pieces of paper and tear examples out of magazines. Create collages that represent ideas for how the content should be developed. As you're making the collages, discuss each asset as you add it and try to decide which work well—or at least try to understand why some team members don't agree on which assets work well and try to resolve those issues right then and there.

The collages provide useful prompt material that you can take into research and see which ideas work, which need to be adapted, and which need to be scrapped.

tip Creating collages on rolls of brown paper (see Figure 4-5) makes them easier to travel with and store.

FIGURE 4-5: A content audit workshop in progress, showing a collage that has been created to represent the project team's content ideas.

RESEARCH TECHNIQUE: Listen to and observe users

For simplicity this research can be done at the same time as the task modeling research. Spend time simply listening to what users say. What questions are they asking? What information is communicated to them that gives satisfactory answers?

Listen to how the responses are being expressed—are there certain words that are being used that seem to be particularly effective? Look for any documentation that's being referred to. Staff in call centers and at help desks frequently have access to, or have created their own, resources for responding to customer needs.

Start to fill in your content requirements document with this information.

We once listened to calls while working on a travel website. A lady called wanting to book a family cruise worth several thousand dollars. She'd been through the process online, but didn't have the confidence to complete the purchase because she couldn't see that her children would be fed nutritional meals each day. We heard several similar requirements and created additional information for the site. Listening to these requirements and making these changes transformed the online success of the business.

RESEARCH TECHNIQUE: Use benchmark testing

Testing an existing service against its competition allows the project team to audit content with users at an early stage in the project. This provides information on what users do and don't understand, the questions they have at the beginning of the task and the questions they still have afterward. Capture the content needs from both the existing service and competitor services and use them to populate the requirements document.

For example, with an e-commerce site, you might uncover that users consistently aren't buying a product on a competitor's site because a key piece of information is missing. You can use this knowledge to ensure that the information is presented on your site.

What's the simplest way to put together a content requirements document?

A content requirements document is the first thing I do at the beginning of every project. It helps me to come to grips with the content, the functionality, and specific words and labels that will be required. Importantly it helps me to understand what I don't know in terms of the industry and the way specific functionality works. Understanding what you don't know helps to give focus to questions for the stakeholder team.

There are a few ways to put together a simple content requirements document and the temptation is to use Excel or Apple's Numbers. However, using an outliner tool—such as Apple's OmniOutliner (see Figure 4-6) or Microsoft Word's outline view—can help you get structure and ideas down quickly without worrying about formatting.

Simply add all the content requirements into the list as they are uncovered, adding descriptive text or example images as necessary.

You can structure the document by grouping similar requirements together (for example, if they are all on the same page of the site), nesting items, and rearranging the order of the items and groups.

FIGURE 4-1 Content requirements can be collated simply in OmniOutliner.

HOW TO Create a content requirements document in Word

Word is an ideal tool to use to create content documents because it handles large tables well (unlike PowerPoint) and images can easily be inserted into individual table cells (unlike Excel).

Setting up the template

Use the following settings to create the maximum document area to work on:

❶ Create a new blank document in Word.

❷ Click the Page Layout tab and set the Orientation to Landscape.

❸ Click Margins and choose Narrow.

Creating the audit

Creating the audit is incredibly simple, but there are a few tricks included in the following descriptions to help create a clean, well-styled document.

Titling the presentation

Add your heading in 24-point type and add your subheadings at 12 points. As shown in Figure 4-7, use 8-point type for the body copy. You can use a larger font if you want to, but 8-point allows you to fit more words into each table cell.

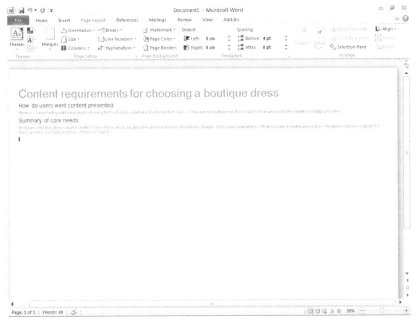

FIGURE 4-7: The title and summary information have been added to the document.

Inserting the table

To insert a table, follow these steps:

1 Click the Insert tab.

2 Click the Table button.

3 Mouse over the grid that's shown in Figure 4-8 to select the number of rows and columns you require.

In this example, the grid is five columns wide and five deep.

FIGURE 4-8: Clicking the Table button displays a grid that can be used to select the number of rows and columns you want your table to have.

Formatting the table

To format the table, follow these steps:

❶ Select the table by clicking anywhere on it and then click the Design tab to style the table.

❷ In the Table Style Options group, make sure only Header Row and Banded Rows are selected.

❸ In the Table Styles group, click the Light Shading style (see Figure 4-9).

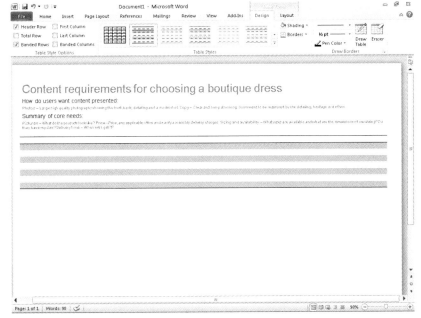

FIGURE 4-9: The light shading button has been selected to give the zebra stripe effect.

You can shade each row individually, but using the preset styles retains the alternating row colors and makes life simpler as more rows are added.

4 Select all the header row cells (the first row) by clicking in the first cell and dragging to the right.

5 In the Table Styles group, click the Shading drop-down arrow and then choose a darker shade of gray. A 35% darker gray is used in the example.

6 Select the entire table again and, in the Table Styles group, click the Borders drop-down arrow.

7 Choose the No Border option.

8 Click into the header row, click the Layout tab, and then in the Data group, click Repeat Header Rows (see Figure 4-10).

note If your document spans multiple pages the header will be displayed on each.

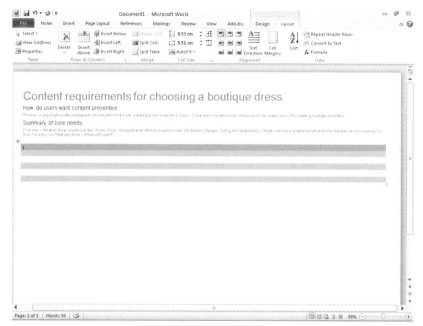

FIGURE 4-10: The borders have been removed and the header row has been given a darker shade of gray.

❾ Type the header text using 8-point type. The example uses a 15% lighter than black shade for all the content.

❿ Mouse over the column borders and drag them to the right or left to set the width of each column.

Figure 4-11 shows a clean-looking table that can now be populated with content.

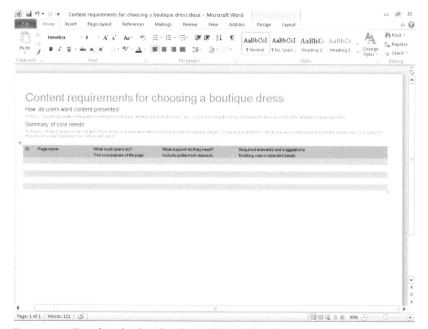

FIGURE 4-11: The column headings have been added and the table is ready to be used.

Adding content

Creating the audit is simply a matter of populating the cells in the template with the content requirements as you uncover them.

Inserting images helps to visualize the requirements, so it's worth including them where you can (see Figure 4-12). To insert an image, click the Insert tab then click the Picture button.

If you need to add additional rows or columns, you can right-click in any cell and use the menu to add rows above or below or add columns to the right or left of the one you are in.

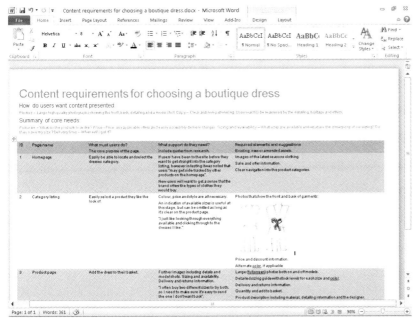

FIGURE 4-12: The finished document with content requirements added.

chapter 5

Sitemaps

A SITEMAP IS an important document for tying all project documents together. It shows the structure of the site and how each page will be linked together during development. It acts as a To Do list to show what wireframes need to be produced. It can be used to map out user journeys and to form the basis of content audits.

In this chapter, you'll learn the information a sitemap (see Figure 5-1) should contain and how to present it in a clear concise way. You'll also learn how to do this based on the type of site you are developing, and the different team members it will be presented to. There are techniques for designing the document as well as techniques for researching and organizing data.

There are also guides on how to create sitemaps in Excel, Word, and OmniGraffle.

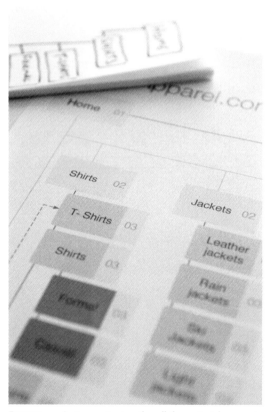

FIGURE 5-1: A sitemap ties together all the project documents.

What makes a good sitemap?

A good sitemap shows the navigation structure and key pages of a website. It should never be a complete map of your website. If you map out every page exactly, the document will become out of date very quickly. Think about when you look at where you live in the Google satellite view; the image is always old, the car you owned two years ago is on the street, or a house two doors down has not yet been built yet. Full-scale maps are very hard to keep up to date.

A full map of every page of a site could also become vast and unmanageable. Imagine trying to map out Amazon.com. A sitemap should focus on the top navigation, the subnavigation categories, and tertiary navigation levels. For a clothing website, you would map out your main product types (shirts, trousers, shoes, and so on). You would then categorize each product type according to style (casual shirts, dress shirts, and so on). But you wouldn't delve into specific product pages.

What the sitemap needs to do is show the main structure of the site and also provide the project team with a checklist of all the key templates that need to be produced. It shows you what templates need to be produced, and where everything sits in relation to each other.

> **note** The sitemap ties a lot of other project documents together, showing which wireframes are used for which section of the site and which are being used to map out user journeys. So a good sitemap needs show a clear reference to other relevant project documents.

When to create a sitemap

There are three key scenarios that require a sitemap to be created.

When you need to audit your current content

If you need to get an idea of the current state of your site, then mapping it out gives you a great overview. It will show you what pages you currently have and if it is structured in the right order. A sitemap can also form the basis of a more detailed content audit.

When you need to enhance or improve your current site structure

This scenario could be a project that just focuses on reorganizing the site structure, or part of an overall design overhaul. The best way to start a project like this is to map out the pages and structure that currently exist. Use that to determine what pages exist, what's missing, and what can be removed before restructuring content.

When you are creating a new website

If you are creating a new website, a sitemap can provide you with a clear plan of action for what needs to be produced. The site structure needs to be thought out before wireframe production begins because it can help determine what templates and content need to be produced. See Figure 5-2.

FIGURE 5-2: Use Post-Its to sketch out the sitemap so you can quickly try out different site structures.

What are you communicating?

A sitemap needs to show the pages that support the user goals and the pages that are necessary to meet the business goals. It needs to show the structure of these key pages and the labels for the navigation. The labels you use should reflect the users' needs and use language with which your users are familiar. Avoid industry or internal jargon. For example, a clothing retailer might have cheaper products that are known to everyone within the business as *White label shoes*. Everyone in the business will understand what this means, but customers won't.

A sitemap is used as a To Do list for many members of the project team. It shows them how many unique page templates need to be produced. You might have several pages in your sitemap that share the same template. For example, the shirts, trousers and shoes pages might all share the same template for listing products. To make it clear which pages share a template, every template should be assigned a unique number. Each page in the sitemap should show the number of the template it uses.

Showing key cross-links can be useful on a sitemap. A cross link is when one page links to another, but the pages don't sit within the same navigation category. You should only focus on one or two important examples. Showing every possible cross-link in the site will turn the sitemap into an impenetrable web of lines and arrows. The majority of cross-links can be documented within the wireframes instead.

Show if there are any changes to pages if the user is logged in. Do the users see a different version of the home page? Do they go to an entirely different section of the site all together? It's important to visually separate any logged in areas of the sitemap so the developers can understand which users get access to which pages.

You might need to produce a few different versions of a sitemap to represent the different phases of development. The initial release of a website might have limited pages and functionality, but will have more added in future releases. It's useful to show how new pages will be tied in as the site develops over time.

Sitemaps are not used to show how users will move through your website. They might have been used for this purpose 10 years ago when it was common to think that users came to your site through the homepage and worked their way down though the site in a linear fashion. Nowadays users can enter your site at any point and jump around it sporadically. Sitemaps show how a site is structured and built, not necessarily how users move through it.

A sitemap is a very political document. It is the document that gets the most exposure across the business and everybody has a stake in it. Different departments of a business will want to make sure they are getting the exposure they want, and that the labels that are given are correct. SEO teams want to make sure there are enough spaces in the site for Google-friendly content. UX teams want to make sure it reflects the needs of the users. The key is to make sure you get all the stakeholders' input early on to make sure you can reflect their needs where possible, or give a good reason when you can't.

Who is the audience?

The sitemap needs to reflect the information needs of each of its key audience members.

Wireframers and designers

A sitemaps does two things for wireframers and designers:

> It shows what unique templates need to be produced. Your sitemap needs to show which pages share the same template. The home page might be one template; there might be several second-level category pages that all share the same template. Show this by placing a template number on each page in the sitemap. Pages that share the same template should have the same template number.

> It shows what navigation areas need to be designed into each page. It will also be used as a guide for page titles and navigation labels within the designs. This means it's important to carefully consider what you label each page in the sitemap. Do not use generic names like *Category page 01* or internal jargon labels like *White label products*. Make sure your labels reflect the goals of your users and use language they are familiar with.

Content teams

Content teams want to know what needs to be produced to support your proposed sitemap. If your sitemap contains lots of new pages, it needs to show which pages have existing content and which need to have new content produced.

Development teams

Development teams need to know what templates are to be developed. They also need to know how the whole site links together as well as the structure for implementing the content management system (CMS) platform.

SEO teams

Search engine optimization (SEO) teams want to make sure there is enough space for SEO content within the site and ensure labels are SEO friendly. So the labels you use in the sitemap should reflect the labels that will be used in the final design.

Project managers

More than anyone, project managers want to know what needs to be done (see Figure 5-3). Project managers often have a very high attention to detail and will want to see every page in the sitemap. It's important (for larger, CMS-based sites) to explain that by including every page, the document would look bloated and unmanageable. It's more important to focus on the main structure and key templates.

FIGURE 5-3: Sitemaps are used by project teams as a To Do list, showing how many unique page templates need to be produced.

Different styles of sitemaps

The style of sitemap you produce will depend on the type of site you're planning, the size of the site you're planning, and the people who will be using it.

> A spreadsheet sitemap is a list of the key pages in your site that have been organized and grouped in a tree structure. If you are planning a larger, CMS-driven site, use the spreadsheet style. This is simply because mapping out a larger site visually becomes complex and difficult to read. I've also worked with project managers and developers who prefer a spreadsheet style simply because it matches the way they work.

> A visual sitemap is composed of lines and boxes. This type of sitemap is better suited for smaller sites and for people who think in a visual way.

It's always worth asking those who will be using this document what style is most useful to them.

The anatomy of a spreadsheet sitemap

This section explains the information you need to include in a spreadsheet sitemap and how to present the information clearly. See Figure 5-4.

FIGURE 5-4: Spreadsheet sitemaps use a tree structure and shading to clearly show where each page sits within the site.

Use a tree structure

Using a tree structure makes it easy to see which pages sit within which pages. Put your top navigation in the first column, the secondary level navigation in the next column, and so on.

Add a column to specify template numbers

The project team needs to know how many unique templates to produce. Assign a number to each page that represents the template that the page uses. If multiple pages use the same template, they will have the same number.

Include a notes column

A notes column will allow you to add helpful information for the designers and developers. It's useful to add notes about areas that are reserved for logged in users, pages that cross link to other areas of the site, and pages that are intended for main navigation or footer links.

Use flags for non-existent content

Highlight pages that do not yet have the content available. This helps the project manager and content team understand how much content they need to produce.

Use actual labels

When you hand your sitemap to designers, chances are they will take the labels used in your sitemap and use them in their designs. It's important to finalize the page labels at the sitemap stage; it's much easier to amend a page name on a sitemap than it is to amend it on the final designs.

Use shading for visual grouping of navigation categories

By using shading, you can better show the groups of navigation categories making it easier for users to see the different sections. Figure 5-4 shows that light gray is used to distinguish one Level 2 category (for example, Shirts) from another Level 2 category (Jackets), and so on. It's best to use a light gray to separate sections; darker colors or outlines tend to create visual clutter.

The anatomy of a visual sitemap

This section explains the information needed for a visual style sitemap and how to present the information clearly. See Figure 5-5.

Don't make your connecting lines too dark

Your connecting lines are important, but the visual priority should be on the page labels. If you use thick, black lines, your sitemap can look cluttered. Use a mid-gray line that is easy to see but isn't so strong that it detracts from the page labels.

Use shading to show levels

When a lot of pages are displayed on a sitemap it can be difficult to see how deep within the navigation structure some pages are. Shading can combat this. Use a light color for your top page (for example, your Home page). Every time you create another level of navigation, use a darker color. The deeper you delve into the structure, the darker the pages get.

Show key cross-links

If you need to show how users can jump from one section of the site to another, it's important to use a different line style and color from the usual navigational routes. This will tell the reader that it's not part of the main site structure and that it's an alternative route between pages.

Use template numbers

It's important to show how many pages will need a unique template to be designed and developed. The example sitemap has 43 pages, but most of these share a template, so only 15 templates need to be produced. The numbers you assign to these pages should be included in the wire frame document, so the developer knows what templates are to be used for each page.

Separate logged in areas

If certain areas of the site are available only to some users (for example, those with accounts), these areas should be flagged. A dotted line around these pages is usually used to show logged-in areas.

Flag non-existent content

Highlight pages that do not yet have the content available. This helps the project manager and content team understand how much content they need to produce.

Use actual labels

Designers are likely to use the labels in your sitemap in their designs. It's important to finalize page labels at the sitemap stage. It's much easier to change a page name on a sitemap than it is on the finished page templates.

Visually differentiate other content types

Some pages in your sitemap might link to downloadable content or trigger an email. You need to represent these differently from the standard pages using icons. This is so the project team knows if other content (such as emails and downloadable PDFs) need to be produced.

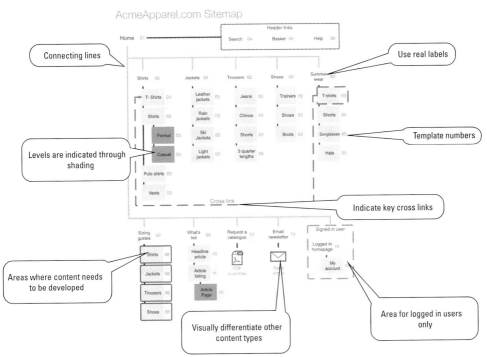

FIGURE 5-5: Visual sitemaps use boxes and lines to show connections between pages. The placement of boxes and the use of shading shows the structure.

RESEARCH AND WORKSHOP IDEAS

This section explains techniques for work-shopping and researching ways to organize your pages and to determine what pages need to be included in your site.

RESEARCH TECHNIQUE: Use site analytics and search logs

If you have to create a new sitemap for an existing site, the chances are people can't find what they want on the current site. Site analytics are a great way to show what areas of your site are working well and what is performing not so well. In terms of informing a sitemap, use site analytics to determine where people are currently going in your site, and where they are not going. This should broadly show you what navigation labels and structures are encouraging people to dig deeper into your site.

However, analytics can't tell you *why* people are visiting certain areas of the site and not others. Analytics might show a certain page to be very popular, but is this because it's what people wanted to see? Or are your navigation labels sending a lot of users to the wrong place? Analytics can't get you the reasoning behind user behavior. It's important to run user testing to understand why people take certain routes through your site and what your navigation labels mean to them. Analytics help you understand what's going on; user testing helps you understand why it's happening.

Search logs are really useful for choosing navigation labels. People use search bars on most websites when they can't find what they want by browsing. So if a user is looking for a certain product on your site, and none of the navigation labels you've come up with help him find it, he will type a term in the search bar that he thinks best represents what he's looking for. The great thing about this is that you should have a ton of terms that real people use to describe your products or areas of your site. So you don't have to guess what words your users are thinking—you have it all written down. If you have a high volume of search terms for a specific area or product, then you can use the most common term as your label.

Card sorting (see Figure 5-6) is a great way to create a site structure that reflects the way users think about your website. It also ensures you create navigation labels in language users are familiar with. This is because card sorting is essentially an exercise that gets users to create a sitemap for you.

To run a card-sorting session, write the name of every page from your site or every product in your stock onto a separate piece of card stock. Lay all of these out onto a table and then bring a test participant in to organize them for you. A card-sorting session is around one hour long—any longer and the participant starts to lose interest. The goal of this session is for the participant to group cards together in a way that he feels is logical. For example: does he put shoes and boots in one group, and trousers and shorts in another group? Once all the cards have been organized into groups, the participant must name each group he created. This is the bit that participants usually find most difficult and you will usually find that the act of trying to put a name to a group causes them to do a final bit of re-organizing (which is fine). Also it's quite common for participants to create a group called "other stuff." It's important to note the pages or products that the user had difficulty grouping, but you should encourage him to try to group them into other sections.

FIGURE 5-6: Open-card sorting invites users to organize your website in a way that makes sense to them.

Six to 12 card-sorting sessions is usually enough for a project. The goal at the end of all these sessions is to see common groupings across participants. Did everybody group the same sets of products together? Did participants use the same labels to describe groups?

There is some really useful software that allows you to input all your data from card-sorting sessions and then group the data in a number of ways for you to analyze. For example, xSort for Mac not only allows you to analyze data but also run card-sorting sessions using digital cards that participants drag around the screen with their mouse.

One of the most common ways to use software to show themes from card sorts is through dendrograms (cluster trees). A *dendrogram* is a tree diagram that shows how closely related items in your card sorts are, based on an average of each session. The more times two items are grouped together, the closer they will appear in the dendrogram. The farther apart two items appear in the dendrogram, the less your participants thought they were related.

It's possible to do card sorting remotely using online tools like WebSort.net. This is great for getting a high volume of results. However, it's always worth running some of the sessions as face-to-face interviews. Interviews allow you to find out why things are grouped together and why some things are difficult to categorize. If participants do not understand what some of the pages are, you can explain it to them and ask how they would describe it more clearly. This means you can make sure your products and pages are described correctly and that your navigation and groupings will work.

The dendrogram shown in Figure 5-7 shows that participants thought T-shirts were closely related to polo shirts, not so related to vests, and completely unrelated to boots, shoes, and trainers.

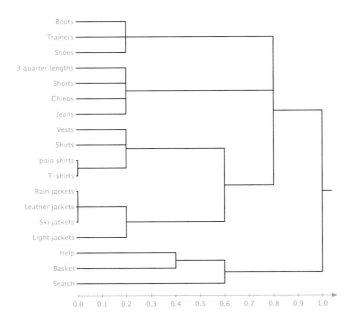

FIGURE 5-7: Analyzing a dendrogram.

RESEARCH TECHNIQUE: Determine the pages you need

If you are creating a sitemap for a website that does not exist yet, then the sitemap does not just show how the pages are structured, but what pages need to be included. The business will always have a strong idea of what they want to include in their website.

To a get clear idea of what the business wants in the site you'll need to interview all the key stakeholders. Every department in the business will want to make sure its needs from the website will be supported. It's easy to assume that an e-commerce site will simply be made up from all the products it sells, but it's very common for business to want editorial sections with articles and blogs to help boost its brand and SEO rankings.

You also need to determine what content your users will need from your new website. The structure and labeling users expect will come out of the card-sorting sessions. First it's helpful to find out what content they will expect and find helpful. The best way to do that is through benchmark testing (see Figure 5-8), which involves recruiting participants who use services similar to the one your website will be providing. Get them to perform tasks on competitors' websites. The aim is to find out what tasks they go to these sites for and how well your competitors support these tasks. You can then either be influenced by the structure and content they provide, or learn from their failings.

FIGURE 5-8: Benchmark testing helps you see if other websites are structured in ways that users understand.

RESEARCH TECHNIQUE: Validate your sitemap

Once have created a sitemap and navigation based on business requirements and user goals, you need to make sure the site structure works before you start coding.

Closed-card sorts

Closed-card sorts are the same as open-card sorts, but use a specified number of groups that have pre-determined names (usually tied to top-level navigation). This is why they are more suited to validating your navigation structure.

Closed-card sorts are run much in the same way as open-card sorts, with every page written on a card. However, also write a card for each label of your top navigation, place those on the table, and tell participants that they are to use those as their groups.

By using closed-card sorting, you're trying to determine if participants understand the labels you have used in your top navigation. If they have, then great—they can stay the same. If not, then ask yourself, "What did they think they meant? What language would they use to describe each group instead?" You also want to see if they put all the pages in the same groups as you did on your sitemap. If the results match your navigation structure, it's working in a way that makes sense to users. If the results don't match, you need to restructure your sitemap.

Remote navigation testing

Remote navigation testing is a cheaper and faster way to validate your sitemap and navigation. This is because they are un-moderated and multiple tests can take place at once.

Online tools like PlainFrame (see Figure 5-9) and Treejack are used for these tests. They work by entering your site structure into the tool and then setting tasks based around finding specific pages—for example, "find short trousers." It's always a good idea to set a number of tasks that require the users to look in all areas of your structure. It's important not to focus the tasks on the easy-to-find pages. If there was a particular page that was difficult for you to categorize, then that should form part of your test.

Once your tasks are set, email a link to the test to your participants. They will be asked to complete each task on your navigation one by one. The outcome is a list of results based on whether or not participants were able to complete the tasks. If participants were able to find what they were looking for, the navigation is working. If participants were not able to find a page, these tools tell you where they tried to look. This tells you where people expect to find certain pages, so you should restructure your sitemap to match these expectations.

Remote navigation testing is great for seeing if the navigation is working with a high number of participants. It's still worth conducting face-to-face card sorts so you can talk to participants about why they might be having difficulty completing some tasks.

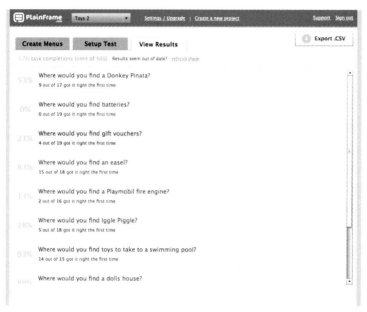

FIGURE 5-9: Remote testing tools tell you if participants successfully used you navigation.

What's the simplest way to create a sitemap?

To create a quick and simple sitemap I always find it best to use the Outline view in Microsoft Word. It allows you to quickly add all your pages into a list and organize them into a tree structure. The simple nature of Outline view means you only concentrate on the structure of the sitemap and not about how the document looks, which is important if you are pressed for time.

I like to start a sitemap in Outline view even if I intend to create a more visual version of it later. It's a great way to plan out the structure of the document before you try to add any styling to it.

To create a sitemap in Outline view, simply open up a new Word document, click View, and then click Outline. Once you are in Outline view, simply start typing all your pages. Press Enter every time you add a new page. Indent pages that sit within others to create your tree structure. In Figure 5-10, Jeans and Chinos each lives within Trousers. To change the indent in outline view, use Tab or Shift+Tab (this works on PC and Mac).

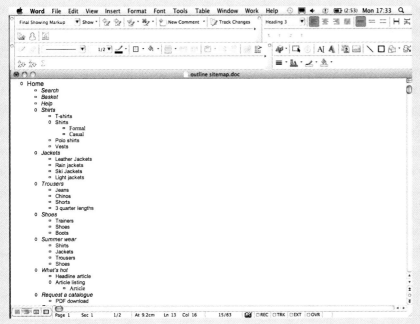

Figure 5-10: Outline view allows you to quickly plan out a site structure.

HOW TO Create a sitemap in PowerPoint

In this section, you'll learn how to create a sitemap using PowerPoint, including shaded shapes and connecting lines.

Setting page orientation

When creating sitemaps in PowerPoint, the slide orientation you use depends on the structure of your sitemap. If it's a deep structure (long and thin), a portrait layout is needed. If it a wide structure, landscape is more appropriate.

To change the orientation, go to the Design tab, click Slide Orientation option. This tutorial will use the Landscape orientation (see Figure 5-11).

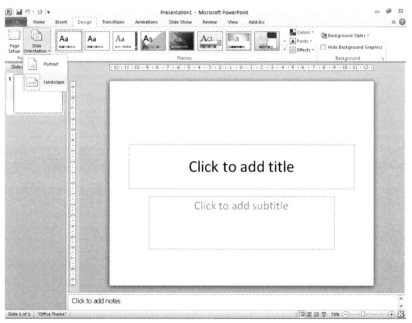

FIGURE 5-11: The orientation of the slide will depend on how many pages you need to include in your sitemap.

Creating and shading boxes

A box will represent each page in the sitemap. To create one, go the Home tab, click the Shapes drop-down, and then select the Rounded Rectangle. Whether you use rounded corners or not is really personal preference; they do tend to soften the look of the document, so you should consider using them.

To reduce the visual clutter on the page, don't use outlines on any of the boxes; just use a light Shape Fill for your first box (see Figure 5-12). You can access additional colors by clicking More Fill Colors.

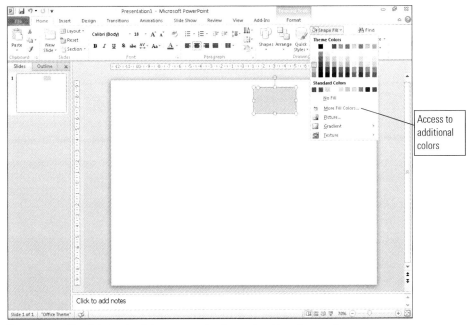

FIGURE 5-12: To minimize visual clutter, use soft colors and avoid outlines on shapes.

Use shading to show how deep in the navigation each page is. Start to create more boxes for your first and second level of navigation. Give the boxes in each new level of navigation a darker shade. It's a good idea to introduce some color at this point (see Figure 5-13) because you might soon run out of varying shades of gray.

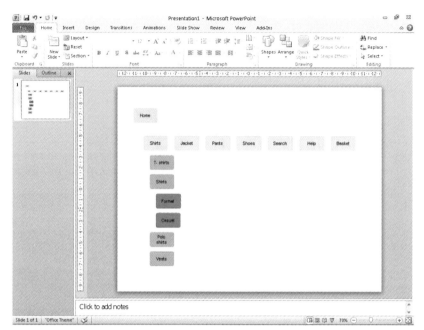

FIGURE 5-13: The top navigation is a light blue, the second level is a darker blue, and the third level is an even darker shade of blue.

Adding connecting lines

To connect two of the boxes together:

❶ Click the Home tab and in the Drawing group, click the Shapes drop-down and select the Elbow Connector.

> **tip** This style of line is best to use because it creates corners in the line to move around objects.

❷ Drag the line from the Home box to one of your second-level boxes.

As shown in Figure 5-14, the line snaps to one of four center points on each box.

❸ Once you've drawn all your lines, use the Shape Outline drop-down in the Drawing group on the Home tab to make your lines a thin mid gray. The lines need to be clearly visible, but must not take attention away from the page boxes.

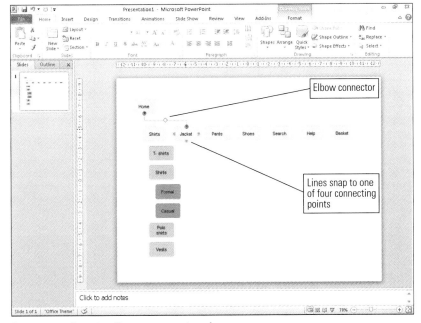

FIGURE 5-14: Snapping elbow connectors into place.

Signifying page groups

Sometimes you will need to show that groups of pages are part of a specific set (for example, when showing logged in pages or footer links). The usual way of showing this is by drawing a box around the group of pages using a dashed outline box

❶ Select a Rectangle from the Shapes drop-down in the Drawing group on the Home tab.

❷ Use the Shape Fill drop-down to remove the fill.

❸ Use the Shape Outline drop-down to set the outline to a thin gray dashed line, as shown in Figure 5-15.

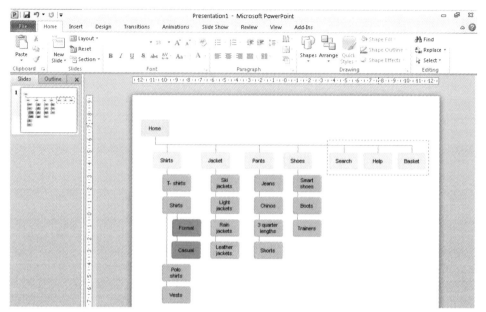

FIGURE 5-15: Dashed outlines are used to signify logged in areas of the site.

Showing cross-links

To show when two pages in the site are linked together, but not as part of the main structure of the site, use a visibly different style of line—known as a *cross-link*—to connect them. For example, use an elbow connector with an arrow on one end to link the two pages (see Figure 5-16). This shows the direction of the cross-link. Click the Shape Outline drop-down to change the line to a bright color and a dash; this visually differentiates it from the other connecting lines.

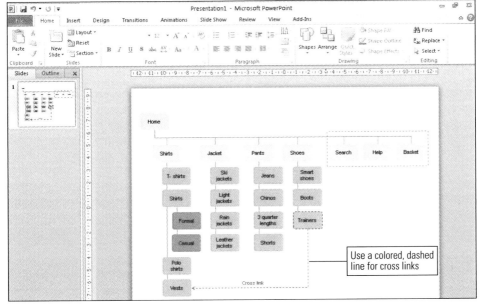

FIGURE 5-16: Cross-links should look different from normal navigation paths.

HOW TO Create a sitemap in OmniGraffle

To produce sitemaps in OmniGraffle, you must create a couple of key elements you need to create and you must follow the same structure that you learned in the section entitled "Anatomy of a Visual Sitemap."

Setting up the template

The way your page is laid out depends entirely on the structure of the sitemap. If it has a narrow top navigation with deep sets of pages, use a portrait setup. If it has a wide top navigation with shallow sets of pages, use a landscape setup.

It's best to design for a large format print out where possible. This gives you more room to maneuver and creates a much easier document to digest.

Creating boxes with magnetic points

To create boxes with magnetic points, follow these steps:

1. On the Toolbar above the canvas, click the Shape button and then select a rectangle.

2. Draw a rectangle on your canvas.

3. Using the style section of the inspector, apply a shaded fill and remove the outline and shadow (see Figure 5-17). This eliminates unnecessary lines and clutter from the sitemap.

4. Duplicate this shape for every page in your sitemap and organize them into the site structure. User a darker shade for each level of navigation you create. (See Figure 5-18.)

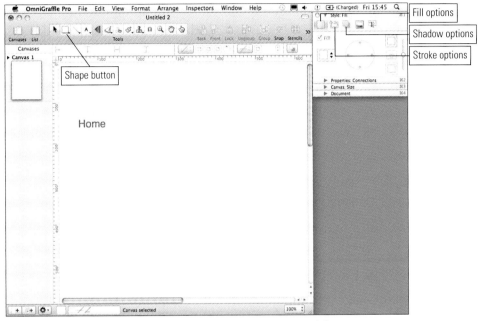

FIGURE 5-17: Remove lines and shadows from your shapes to remove visual clutter.

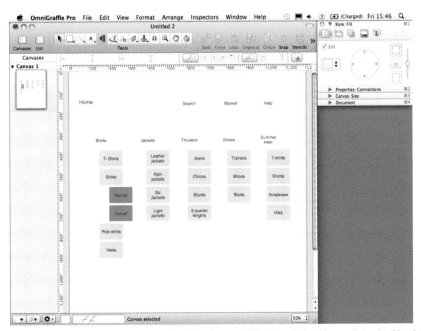

FIGURE 5-18: The top navigation is a light blue, the second level is a darker blue, and the third level is an even darker shade of blue.

❺ Select all your rectangles, go to the Properties section of the inspector, and then select the Connections option.

❻ Make sure the Allow connections from lines checkbox is selected.

❼ Set the magnets drop-down to 4 magnets N, S, E, W (as shown in Figure 5-19). This makes it easier to connect lines between two rectangles.

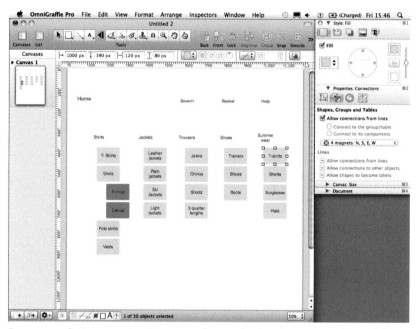

FIGURE 5-19: Setting magnetic points on your shapes makes it easier to connect them with lines.

Using connecting lines

To use connecting lines, follow these steps:

❶ On the Toolbar above the canvas, click and hold the Line Tool button (see Figure 5-20).

❷ Select the Orthogonal Stroke: Obsidian line tool. This line creates corners that move around objects.

❸ Draw a line from one of the rectangles to the other.

As shown in Figure 5-20, small circles appear on the rectangle. These are the magnet points, and lines will snap to one of these points every time you draw one either to or from the rectangle. This is really useful for making sure the lines all start from the same position on every box in your sitemap.

❹ Repeat these steps to connect all the pages.

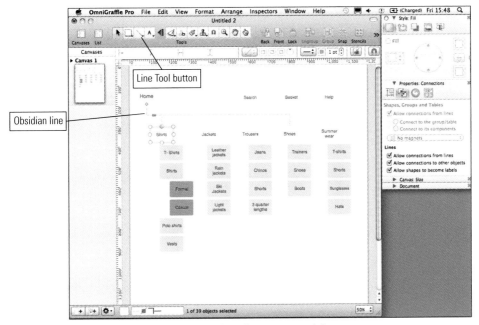

FIGURE 5-20: Orthogonal lines allow you to create lines that move around shapes.

De-magnetizing lines

Sometimes you need you lines to not snap to the magnetic points on your shapes because you want more control over their positions. To de-magnetize lines, follow these steps:

1 Select the line you want to de-magnetize.

2 Click the Magnetize button (see Figure 5-21). When the line is de-magnetized, its end points turn blue.

To finish off your sitemap, add a gray box to the right of each page rectangle (see Figure 5-22) and add the template number. If you need to show cross-links, remember to use a line style and color that is different from your other connecting points.

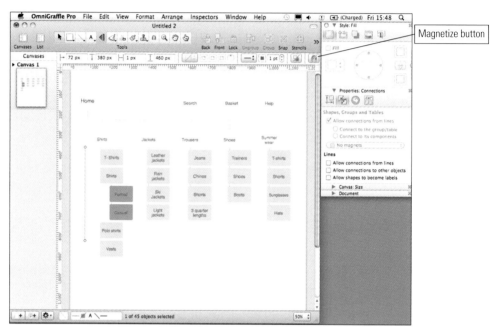

FIGURE 5-21: De-magnetizing lines stops them snapping to shapes.

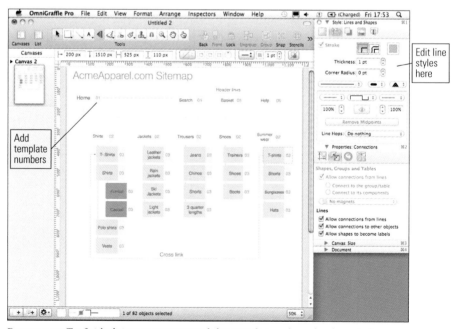

FIGURE 5-22: The finished site map uses repeated elements that you have already created.

HOW TO Create a sitemap in Excel

Here are some simple instructions on how to create the key elements of an Excel sitemap. There are no advanced techniques here—just simple formatting instructions.

Writing labels and wrapping text

To add labels, simply select a cell and type the label. You will find that some labels are longer than their cell width, so the text covers the cells to their right (see Figure 5-23).

> **tip** It's better to get all your page names written at once, before formatting, so you can then format multiple cells at once.

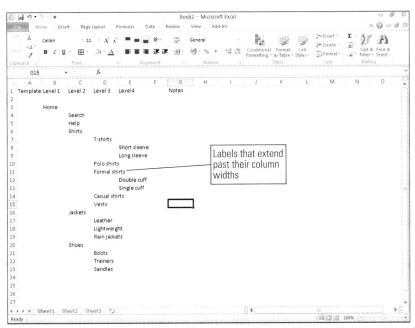

FIGURE 5-23: Labels that extend beyond their column widths.

To fix this problem, you can get the text to wrap within the cell space by following these steps:

❶ Select all the cells using the keyboard shortcut Ctrl+A.

❷ Right-click anywhere in the cells and select Format Cells.

❸ Select the Alignment tab within the Format cells window.

❹ Select the Wrap text check box (see Figure 5-24).

Now if your text is too long for the cell, it wraps onto a new line.

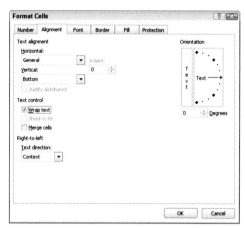

FIGURE 5-24: Enabling the text-wrapping option.

Shading cells

You will need to apply different colors to your sitemap to signify pages that need content to be produced for the final website or to visually organize the information in order to make it easier to read:

❶ Click the cell you want to shade.

❷ On the Home tab, in the Font group, click the Fill Color button and then choose a color (see Figure 5-25).

As shown in Figure 5-25, red shows content that is currently missing from the site.

To shade a group of cells, click and drag across the group of cells you want to shade. Pick a color in the same way. In Figure 5-26, various shades of gray are used to visually group the information without introducing clutter.

You can shade an entire column or row, too. In fact, it's a good idea to use shading for the Notes column and the Template column so they are visually differentiated from the pages in the sitemap. To apply shading to an entire column, click the column letter (see Figure 5-27) and then choose your shading. To apply shading to an entire row, click the row number and then choose your shading.

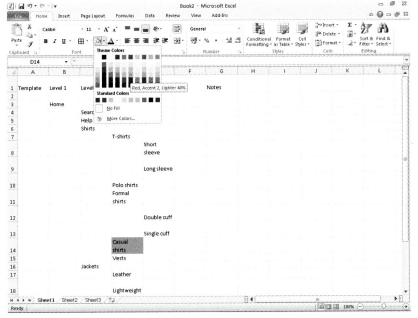

FIGURE 5-25: Select a cell and click the Fill Color button to choose a color.

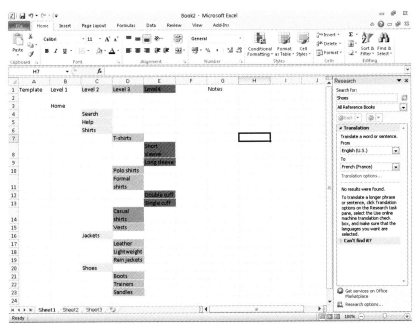

FIGURE 5-26: Use shading to group pages that sit within the same categories and to emphasize what navigation level they sit in.

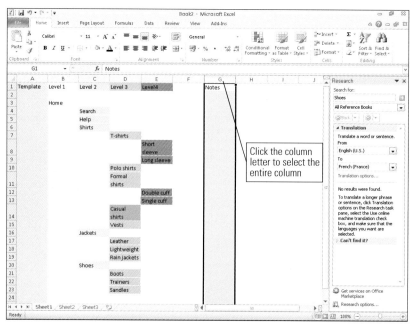

FIGURE 5-27: Selecting an entire column.

Adding new rows and columns

To add new rows or columns in the middle of you sitemap:

1 Click the cell directly below where you want to add a row or directly left of where you want to add a column.

2 Right-click and then choose Insert.

3 In the Insert dialog box, select Entire row or Entire column.

To add multiple rows or columns:

1 Select number of cells that match the number of rows or columns you want to add. For example, to add three new rows, select the three row numbers below where you want to add these new rows.

2 Right-click the selected rows and choose Insert.

3 In the Insert dialog box, select Entire Row.

In the example shown in Figure 5-28, a new row is being inserted below Row 6.

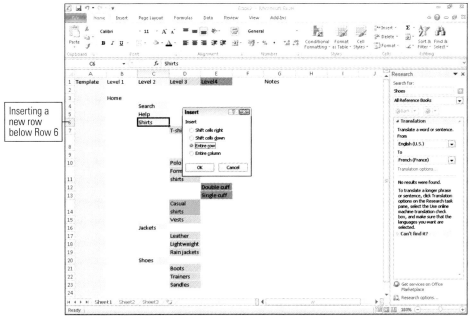

Inserting a new row below Row 6

FIGURE 5-28: Inserting a new row.

Wireframes

6

GOOD WIREFRAMES CAN transform a project. Like an engineer's blueprint or an architect's drawings, wireframes become the glue that holds the product, technical, design, and management teams together. And they are perfect to get in front of your audience to validate that the ideas work.

At the end of this chapter you'll look at developing wireframes using specific tools, but the principles discussed can be used in any software. See Figure 6-1.

What makes a good wireframe?

Wireframes allow the entire project team to focus on the interface that is being created. You can consider if the product or service is being presented in the right way, how the content will be structured, where the data will come from, how the functionality will be developed, and visually how the page will be laid out and where the emphasis is required.

To help focus on user experience qualities such of ease of use, simplicity, and friendliness, our colleague Giles Colborne has developed a three-level order of importance:

> **How does it feel?** Does the user interface respond and act as the user wants it to? Reinforcing users' tasks and enhancing their expectations of the product.

> **How does it look?** Is the interface design clear and well structured?

> **How does it work?** This is the technical implementation that is needed to support the look and feel.

For the user, feel is more important than look (as the system first needs to match how a user wants and needs it to behave), which is more important than how it works (users are happy when things just work, not necessarily how they work).

It's a useful framework for assessing your work and prioritizing elements. And it's also a good reminder that while the wireframe is a very functional document (majoring on the look and workings), the prize is on getting the feel right for the users.

This chapter focuses primarily on static wireframes and what needs to be communicated in them to help improve the documents you produce. Of course, these can then be made interactive as required.

<small>FIGURE 6-1: A wireframe document showing the page with callouts referring to notes.</small>

When to create a wireframe?

Some form of prototyping should be used on every project—whether it's a sketch on a piece of paper or a fully blown OmniGraffle, Axure, Visio, or HTML prototype. They make ideas real and give focus and direction to the problems you are trying to resolve.

A good wireframe is born out of a collaborative process. The whole project team should be involved from the first sketches through to the final document delivery. Review meetings should be frequent — one of the benefits of prototyping is that alternative ideas and changes are quick to try and discuss.

Get the wireframes in front of the users often and validate that they are working as planned. Again changes are quick to implement and you can validate again if necessary.

What are you communicating?

A well-presented wireframe helps the project team understand the ideal design and functional solution. It's a key piece of UX documentation that is relatively quick and cost effective to produce and yet helps crystallize the product. The following sections describe the elements you want to be discussing.

Vision

Wireframes provide the vision for the site that you are creating. Include the vision objectives at the beginning of the wireframes (and reinforce at the beginning of meetings) to focus and align the team.

Layout

You can organize the structure of the page and where the different elements fit. You can easily try and test alternative layouts to see which works best for the users.

Content and images

What are the content and image requirements for each page? Where will you source the assets from?

Priority

Wireframes help identify what the priority or key element of each page should be. Where do you want users to look? What do you want them to do?

Navigation

How is a user going to move around the site? The wireframes let you try and test different approaches for navigation.

Functionality

Wireframes help identify the functionality of a page. How should users interact with the page and what happens when they do? This will be implied through the affordance—does it look the way it works?—of the elements used, notes, and storyboards.

Who is the audience?

Involving a wide range of stakeholders in the wireframes development enables you to discuss content and functionality without the additional comments on colors, styling, and imagery that you'd have when presenting creative content.

Wireframes get more attention than any other deliverable you develop. This section covers a full list of the roles you will likely work with.

This can seem overwhelming, so it's good practice to agree on the stakeholder sign-off process and ensure that the right people are involved at the right time.

The following sections break such a list into common groups. Remember, every company is different, and that will be reflected in the team you work with. See Figure 6-2.

FIGURE 6-2: Take time to work through the detail of the wireframes with the project team, ensuring it meets the business requirements and can be developed.

Development team

The development team group is directly involved with the development and release of the product.

> **Designers** want to understand the content needs, visual hierarchy, and how you intend the user to interact. Designers can work on concepts as you're working on wireframes in order to collaborate on the final visual approach. You'll want to avoid them feeling like they are coloring in your work and instead get them to trust that you can architect their creative ideas.

> **Developers** need to understand how the functionality works, both in the front and back ends:

  • With front-end developers you can explore approaches to layout, content organization, and responsive interactions (how something behaves or feels when you interact with it).

  • With back-end developers you can discuss how you can manipulate the data between the user and the database—the wireframes help give focus to these discussions.

- If a content management system (CMS) or e-commerce platform is being used, then having a walkthrough of how it works and seeing examples of implementations will be necessary before you start working on the wireframes.

> **Project managers** want to make sure that agreed-on functionality is in place and that the site can be built by the team on time and on budget. They will know and understand the aims and business reasons for the project and so can give good feedback throughout the wireframe development.

> **Business analysts** will be looking at the detail. They will document what you are creating to the front- and back-end development teams (usually in the form of a functional specification). You'll spend a lot of time with them going through the details.

> **User experience peers** can help you share ideas and liaise with the other team members. You can collaborate with them on techniques and best practices. If you are an agency or individual working with them for the first time, it's worth spending time to understand the standards and approaches they use internally.

Specialists

If available, members of the specialists group will add to the quality of the thinking in your wireframes. Carrying their input into the wireframes is of huge value to the subsequent development and roll-out of the product and ensures less amends later.

> **Search engine optimization (SEO) teams** are interested in seeing the navigation and content layout and offering input on them. Getting these specialists involved early in the wireframe development ensures that the SEO needs of the site will be in place from launch.

> **Content and copy teams** want to understand how elements will appear on the site and link together. They will be responsible for writing or commissioning new content for the site and ensuring that all elements have a consistent tone of voice.

> **Analytics specialists** are looking at conversion paths and areas where the site needs to be optimized. They may have good insights from existing analytics, which help shape the flow of the site. They may also be responsible for multi-variant testing (MVT), looking at layout scenarios to test after launch.

> **Accessibility teams** want to know that the site can be developed using clear semantic markup and that complex interactive elements can degrade gracefully. They are interested in the clarity of the copy and that the designs work for users with colorblindness.

Related business functions

Related business function teams often have responsibilities outside of the project, but their views and opinions are of critical importance to the direction of the wireframes.

> **Product managers** want to see their ideas realized and make sure that you've encapsulated the benefits of the product accurately. For an e-commerce site, the product managers may understand the monetary value of page elements. It's worth picking their brains on this before you move or remove page elements.

> **Brand and marketing teams** want to ensure that the site is in line with the product and brand vision. Depending on the project they may be liaising with teams across different media to ensure consistency and commissioning market research to ensure consumers respond favorably to the messaging.

> **Legal and compliance teams** can often be seen as a stick applied to your wireframes near the end of the project. However, involving them as stakeholders from an early stage helps you understand their requirements and includes them as part of the deliverable project, ensuring legal sign-off will be a breeze.

> **Finance and operations** can have needs similar to the managing directors, but these folks also will be able to inform the current and future monetization needs of the project and specific products featured.

> **Market researchers** can give information on the audience demographics and have good information on the broad user need of the project.

> **Customer service managers** can provide a wealth of information on users' content needs and specific problems or difficulties that they frequently hear from customers. They will be able to provide a good objective view to the wireframes and point out areas that require clarification.

Sign-off groups

The success of the project is of critical importance to your sign-off groups, but they may not have the availability to be involved on a day-to-day basis.

> **Head of online and online managers** will have ultimate responsibility for what goes on the site. They'll be liaising with all the parties involved to ensure that the site can go live and meet the business objectives. They will be reporting progress to the board and will want to ensure that the wireframes are giving the best solution and can be developed as planned.

> **E-commerce teams** are responsible for the merchandising elements of the site. From the wireframes they will want to make sure that people can find and purchase products easily, that the right content is available for each product, and that offers and promotions (including cross-selling and up-selling) are clearly messaged.

> **Managing director and board member** requirements will vary depending on how hands-on they are, but generally they want to ensure that their money is being invested wisely and that the project is meeting the strategic and revenue needs of the company.

Agency teams

Finally, agency teams will often sit alongside the project team to manage the quality and direction of the delivery.

> **Account directors and managers** are responsible for the relationship with the client and are going to want to ensure that the agency is delivering the best possible solution. You'll need to work with them to ensure they understand why your solution is the best one.

> **Strategists and planners** are interested in the broader context of the project. How does it fit into other projects being worked on? How will it link to marketing activities? They want to understand the context of the wireframes against their activity plans.

Anatomy of a wireframe

This section explains everything you need to include in a wireframe to ensure it communicates your ideas effectively. In Figure 6-3, letters A-E refer to notes located to the right of the figure.

Write clear page titles and numbers

Writing understandable page titles and numbers makes it obvious what page to look at when you talk through wireframes with team members over the phone.

Work in actual pixels when possible

Working in actual pixels stops the guess work and makes sure everything will fit in the final design.

3 Product page

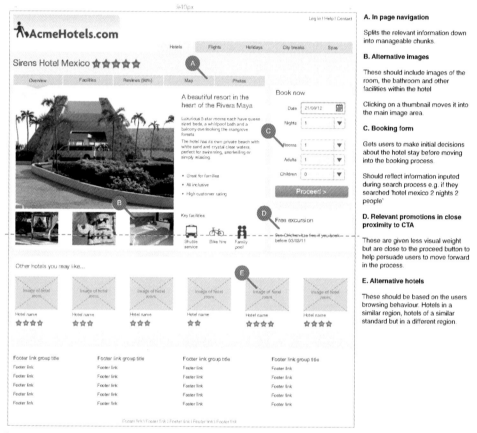

FIGURE 6-3: An example page from a finished deck of wireframes.

Use shading to show visual weighting

Visual prioritization is important to any design. If your wireframes are just made up of white boxes with black outlines, your visual priority will not be communicated to the design team. Use various shades of white and gray to create a visual prioritization.

Avoid black text lines or shapes

Black is harsh on the eyes and makes the page look busy. Use 75% gray text to soften the whole design, and don't use black in shapes.

Use real data

Use product names, prices, navigation labels, filter sets, and phone numbers to ensure all the necessary copy fits in the design. Real data is vital for testing wireframes. Without it testing is unrealistic and you will miss out on users' responses to certain pieces of information.

Use real images where necessary

Use real images to test the wireframes and also to show what style of image needs to be used in the final design.

Write descriptive image placeholders

Images are often the most important part of a website. Simply saying where images must go is not enough. Image placeholders are a great opportunity to describe the type of image to use to enhance the user experience.

Use clear annotation

Describe the functionality and back up your design decisions. Readers of wireframes will be more focused on the designs than the annotation, so keep the annotations short and clear.

Clearly link the notes and wireframes

Use callouts to clearly link notes and wireframes. Deliberately make them a loud color so it's clear they are not part of the design.

Show the fold

Mark what area of your wireframe will be on view when the page first loads and what users will need to scroll to see. This helps to make sure your design gives a cue to users that there is more content for them to view when they scroll down the page.

Other pages to include

This section covers other pages that are included as part of the wireframe document.

Vision

The vision page (see Figure 6-4) is simply a set of design guidelines that you want your wireframes to follow. Having them within your deck of wireframes allows you to constantly check on them and ensure your designs are keeping to the original vision.

1 Vision

Create a simple and helpful site
  Straightforward navigation
  All holiday details in one place
  Be a helpful guide, not a hardcore salesman

Create an easy to use booking process
  Supports user information needs while booking
  Only ask necessary questions

FIGURE 6-4: A vision page reinforces guidelines and project aims.

Change log

To keep the project team up to date with any changes made to the wireframes, you need to log any changes at the start of the document. Otherwise they may be overlooked.

Each entry in the change log (see Figure 6-5) should include the version number of the document, who made the changes (and their contact details), and all the changes made with page references.

This will make it easier for the project team to see the updates without having to scan the entire document.

2 Change log 2

Date	Version	Name	Notes
November 29 2010	0.6	Steve Cable	p3: Added top offers, Added Log in fields, amended search panel p4: Added page for logged in user including home station and favourites p4/p5: Updated search panel to re-include personalised functionality p16: added add to favourites
December 1 2010	0.6	Steve Cable	p6: Added details of favourite products and home page p11: Updated default state of a search results with multiple facets p16: Added details popup p16: Updated the summary to included 'Add to favourites'
December 6 2010	0.8	Steve Cable	p10: Best price panel moved and copy changed Added view switch function (switches between list and grid) p14: Text me details pulled forward, calendar pushed back p19/20: Added user flow and updated the relationship between history and my account
December 7 2010	0.9	Steve Cable	p6: Updated user flow
December 7 2010	1.0	Steve Cable	p6: Updated saved to favourites rules p7: Updated basket overlay matrix: update view switch p22: Added initial rough idea for alternative product page
December 14 2010	1.1	Steve Cable	QTT: Added calendar icons. Updated help text. Removed the delivery time from product listing Matrix: Removed 'highlight. Added the word 'View' to product list items to make function clearer
January 5 2011	1.4	Steve Cable	P14: Updated notes

FIGURE 6-5: A change log helps the team keep track of revisions and who made them.

Storyboards

Certain parts of your wireframe will have functionality that works in a number of steps. Storyboards (see Figure 6-6) allow you to lay those steps out.

Make sure it's clear to the reader what order the storyboard should be read in. People will always read from left to right, but functionality storyboards can sometimes look disjointed and it gets difficult to tell where to look next. Adding guide arrows or numbering can counter this.

Clearly show what users have to do to get to the next step. Do they click a button? Use a drop-down? Highlighting these areas on each step of your storyboard helps clarify the user's path through it.

4 Booking form storyboard

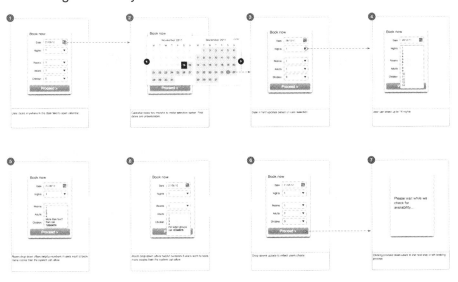

FIGURE 6-6: Storyboards show the team how specific pieces of functionality need to work.

Design principles for wireframes

It is useful to have some base design principles for wireframing. Once mastered, these clarify your documentation and communicate the desired user experience.

Wireframes often have all the information on them but the user experience is not communicated. How should users engage with the content, find what they need, and decide on what they want to do? If these things aren't demonstrated on the wireframe, then it's likely that they won't be communicated to the user when the product is designed and developed.

Structure and style

Creating a clear set of structured elements is the starting point for developing well-presented wireframes.

> Decide on a page grid (see Figure 6-7) that all objects can be aligned to. A 960-px grid is often used because it is divisible by so many numbers—3, 4, 5, 6, 8, or 10 column grids are all possible, for example. We'll show you how to set them up in the "How to..." section of this chapter.

FIGURE 6-7: A page grid helps keep wireframes well structured and aligned.

> Create styles for headings, subheadings, body copy, and links (see Figure 6-8).

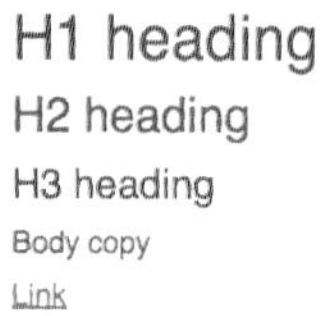

H1 heading
H2 heading
H3 heading
Body copy
Link

FIGURE 6-8: Use a consistent selection of type styles throughout your document.

> Ensure that interactive elements have the appropriate affordance (making them look how they work). For example, make buttons look clickable, as shown in Figure 6-9.

Submit

FIGURE 6-9: Use affordance where necessary to make elements look how they work.

> Use nesting to show how groups of items belong together. This helps a user to understand the structure of your content. Figure 6-10 uses nesting to show the relationship between the different sections of the page. For example, Section 1.3 can clearly be seen to be a child of Section 1.

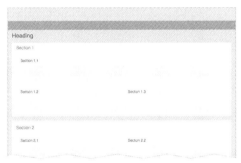

FIGURE 6-10: Nesting gives clarity to which elements belong to each other.

> Finally, be consistent in your use of structure and style between pages.

Visual heat

By using shades of gray you are able to control the emphasis of elements on the page. It helps you to pull out important information and focus users on key messages or calls to action.

This is called visual heat. Here's a simple walkthrough, as shown in Figure 6-11:

❶ Use pale shades of gray to denote the background regions.

❷ Use white blocks on top to focus attention onto the content areas.

❸ Use the darker shades of gray to pull out the text and key calls to action. Black is normally too harsh and will distract the user.

❹ Finally, mid-grays can be used for the remaining elements and lesser calls to action.

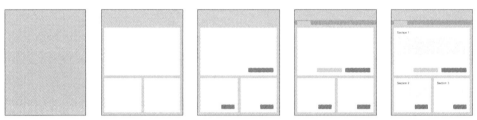

FIGURE 6-11: These images show the buildup of visual heat is created by using different shades of gray.

When to use color

On the whole, color is reserved for indicating the elements to which notes refer (see Figure 6-12).

FIGURE 6-12: A colored marker is used to indicate where notes refer to on the wireframe.

Sometimes color can help to pull out key interaction states such as error messaging, alerts, or other dynamic changes to the interface (see Figure 6-13). However, this can also be done with a darker shade of gray or black.

> Thanks! We've updated your details.

> Thanks! We've updated your details.

FIGURE 6-13: Color can help to reinforce the display and feel of key messages to the user.

Feel

When creating wireframes you are focused on the experience you want the users to have (see Figure 6-14). Often this goes beyond what the page looks like to how you want it to respond as they mouse over and click on elements.

In a static wireframe, there are a few different tricks you can use to document this:

> Storyboard the interaction using clear descriptions with words like fade out, fade in, delay and pause.

> Create a physical mock-up to allow you and others to play with and improve the interaction. Use paper or stick objects to a whiteboard to allow you to move elements around and switch states (see Figure 6-15).

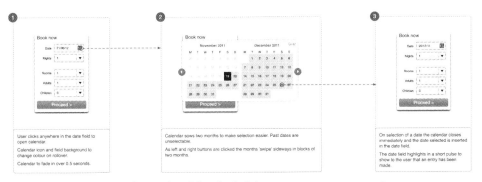

FIGURE 6-14: The captions in this storyboard describe the behavior you want users to experience.

FIGURE 6-15: A physical mock-up shows how an interface will feel to the user.

> Reference existing examples of sites or applications where people have used the same or similar techniques.

> Create simple animations of just the effects—mocking it up in Flash or using HTML and jQuery. The latter can also be useful in assessing how the element will go on to be developed.

Stepping back to help give focus

This is a slightly unusual design principal, but it is a fact that it's easy to get bogged in the process of wireframing (or any creative process for that matter).

Print your images and then spread them out. Imagine yourself clicking through them as a user would; see how the interactions feel (instead of focusing on what they look like).

Also, practice and use the techniques outlined later in the perspective workshops to help regain focus.

Here's a parallel example: while we've been writing this chapter, we've been going back to our initial vision, proposal, and content structure to keep us focused on what it is that we're communicating.

Validating wireframes

Get your wireframes in front of people informally as soon as possible. Friends, family, and colleagues will all help to refine and improve your work. It's never too early to test. Testing a simple sketch on a piece of paper can transform the success of your product.

Carry out formal user testing using the think-aloud protocol on your wireframes at least once during their development. Recruit users that want to perform or are performing tasks the same as the one you are developing. For instance, if you are designing a travel website, recruit people who are currently looking for a holiday. You will be able to test that your ideas are working and refine the language and labeling used.

In most cases, testing on flat non-interactive wireframes (on paper or on screen) is as effective as testing clickable prototypes.

If time or budget is tight, then take the testing to where the users are. We've tested anywhere from cafes to railway stations.

Some tips for wireframe validation:

> If you have used color in your wireframes then ensure that they are gray scaled before testing. It helps you to get a clearer view of whether the emphasis of elements it right.

> Consider removing the logo. Users can be swayed if they know which brand the site is for. If they have a strong affinity with the brand, then they may forgive mistakes; if they don't like the brand, then it can cloud their judgment.

> Use realistic data in your wireframes. Including real product names, prices, and information makes the test more believable for the user. It will ensure the test will prove whether or not users can find the information they need. If the information isn't there (or just represented by placeholder text), then they won't find it.

> Create a flow. Decide what the main journey through your designs is and create the wireframes to support it. Make the journey consistent; for example, if you use a specific product page on an ecommerce site, make sure that product appears in the basket. This will help the test flow better and help spot issues with the journey as a whole, as well as specific pages.

note If the flow of the pages consistently fails to meet the users' expectations, your task model is probably wrong or needs refining (or you haven't developed one). If you don't have a task model, or if you have one but don't stick to it, you'll encounter issues with the wireframes that you are designing.

RESEARCH AND WORKSHOP IDEAS

Each of the following ideas can be used on its own or together as a single workshop.

You'll start with the wireframing process running through all elements, in a single workshop. Then as the wireframes are in development, you'll use one or more of the techniques to help you to step back and make sure that you're on the right track.

Get as many people involved from different aspects of the business as possible. This ensures you capture the requirements and needs up front—my company has run workshops like this with as many as 100 people tweaking the content and facilitation methods where necessary. However, you can se these as exercises by yourself or with a couple of people.

How to run a successful workshop

When you're focusing on wireframes, following these rules will make any workshop you run a better experience for the participants with better outcomes for you.

> The key to a good workshop is planning (see Figure 6-16). Think about the outcome you want to arrive at and then list the activities you need complete in order to get there.

> Develop a list of prompt questions for each activity. You may or may not have your own answers to these already. Either way, the questions will help stimulate discussion and help you to explore a variety of ideas that you're considering.

> Estimate the time each activity will take (you'll get better at this with experience) and stick to your timings. Running through one or all of the activities beforehand will help you to get a sense of this.

> Take time to describe the rules for engagement and set expectations for the workshop. Tell the participants even the simple things like turning off mobile phones, any health and safety notices, how regularly the breaks are going to be, how each activity works, and the outcome you are aiming for.

> It may be your workshop and you'll have ideas about the outcomes, but assume the role of a facilitator. Help people to interact with each other to draw out ideas. Listen for concerns and constraints. Understand previous successes and failures. (See Figure 6-16.)

FIGURE 6-16: Good workshops take planning and preparation.

WORKSHOP IDEA: Prioritize content

This exercise helps you to understand, structure, and prioritize the content required on each page of the site.

① List all the elements you can think of for each page of the site. Putting each one on a Post-It Note (see Figure 6-17) helps you move them around easily.

② Cluster the notes into groups of items that will belong together on the page. For example, on an ecommerce site a quantity button may be linked to the Add to Basket button.

③ Remove duplication.

④ Prioritize these groups. And keep a forced ranking—make sure one group is always above or below another.

⑤ Then, prioritize the items within the groups. Again, make sure that elements don't tie.

6 Finally consider the size, weight, and type of each piece of content.

- Is it a photo, a piece of copy, or a call to action?

- How much space does it need on the page?

- Does it need to appear on the page by default or can it be disclosed or linked to?

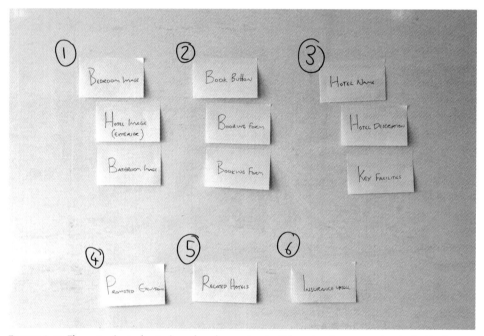

FIGURE 6-17: Elements of a single wireframe have been put onto sticky notes, then grouped and prioritized.

Having gone through this exercise you are left with prioritized groups within which you have prioritized items.

It's useful to put this into a structured list—using Outline View in Word or the excellent Omni Outliner for Mac, for example (although a simple text tool is just as good). This helps to get the semantics right—thinking through what's a heading, a subheading, a copy block, an image, or a link. And you can refer back to it in the future.

Once you have a good shared understanding of the page content you can start to sketch out ideas. There are a number of ways to do this, but my preferred method is to get each person sketching out as many different ideas for solutions as possible in 10 minutes (see Figure 6-18). Then everyone in the group take turns in sharing the ideas and discussing the options.

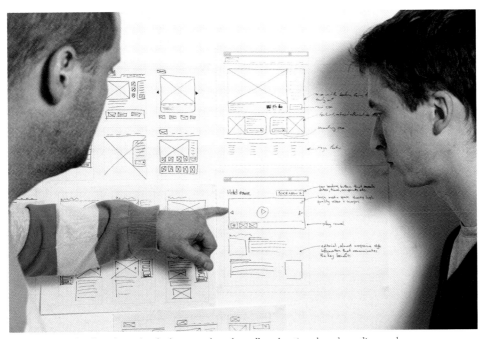

FIGURE 6-18: Ideas have been sketched out, stuck to the wall, and options have been discussed.

As patterns and solutions start to emerge, draw them up on a whiteboard as a group to help reach a consensus of how the final page needs to work.

The sketching workshop is not about getting the design right the first time; rather it's about generating ideas and understanding potential design solutions. The person responsible for wireframes can take the ideas to work up a detailed and considered solution.

It's worth having some tricks up your sleeve to further stimulate ideas:

> Have prompt and stimulus material on hand. Magazines and industry brochures are good to cut up and stick to walls. They'll stimulate discussion on content, layout, and photography.

> Have related business information that may be of use. Analytics data, product information, and business vision documents can all be useful.

> Keep your task models on hand. Going over them again may help develop new ways to consider the structure of navigation and content.

> Walking around towns, workplaces, and stores can help to generate new ideas. For example, use the lunch break to walk around a supermarket to see how the managers have dealt with organization, navigation, promotion, and cross sell. It doesn't need to be directly related — in fact, often it's better if it's not at all related because you want to uncover the unexpected.

> Encourage attendees to take photos of anything they think may be relevant in the week or so leading up to the workshop.

RESEARCH TECHNIQUE: Create a healthy perspective

As you are working on a wireframe deck it's easy to get bogged down with the detail of an individual page. You can forget the context in which it sits and forget the focus of the page itself.

Here are a few workshop ideas to help get over that.

> Sketch out boxes for each of the pages in the user journey (see Figure 6-19). Consider where the page you're currently designing sits. What has the user done before? What is he going to do next? Could a user be deep linking into your page through a search engine? Taking a step back helps to remind you of the purpose of the page.

> Write down a structured list of the elements on the page. What are the headings and subheadings, the key calls to action that you want a user to perform, the content elements? Consider how the elements are grouped together and ordered. This simple task takes you away from the page and refocuses you on priorities.

> If you are familiar with creating, or have an understanding of developing, semantically correct HTML (it's well worth learning if you are not familiar), then apply that knowledge to your wireframes (see Figure 6-20). It will help to focus your mind on the order in which elements appear so that they are as clear and as accessible to your users as possible.

FIGURE 6-19: Sketch out each of the pages to help consider and optimize the flow through the pages.

FIGURE 6-20: Basic HTML tags have been added to the wireframe to help you think through the structure of the page.

> Run a critique session with your colleagues. Project the wireframes onto a whiteboard (see Figure 6-21) and look for ways to refine and optimize the page. Scribble these directly on top of the projection then take a photo of the outcome to have beside you as you work through the changes.

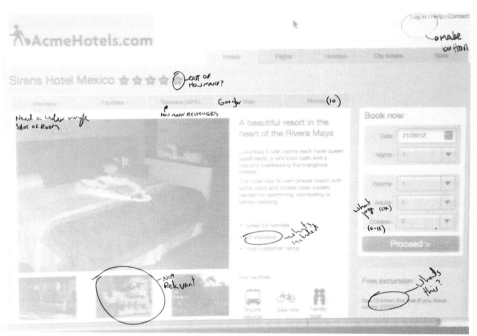

FIGURE 6-21: A wireframe has been projected onto a whiteboard and notes for amends have been sketched over the top.

What's the quickest way to produce a wireframe?

Sketches (see Figure 6-22) are the most obvious way to quickly create and share wireframes. Keeping a notepad and pen to hand means that you can always visualize an idea whether it's for whole page layouts, positioning or broad components or to rethink how a specific function works.

There are a few good digital alternatives now as well, whether it's using:

> Pre-made stencils for OmniGraffle or Axure

> A simpler prototyping tools such as Balsamiq

> A sketching tool such as SketchBook for iPhone or iPad

Sketches are quick to produce and easy to photograph and share.

The beauty of rapid sketching is that you quickly have something to share with the team without anyone thinking it's the finished solution — this can often encourage more honest input.

If you are not physically in the same location, then you can share immediately using a camera phone and email. I've had phone calls where I'll be sketching solutions based on the conversation then emailing them over to talk them through a minute later.

HOW TO Create wireframes in OmniGraffle

This section of the chapter guides you through creating a wireframe in OmniGraffle. It starts by explaining how to set up a template then describes how to create the basic elements that go into creating a wireframe.

First, become familiar with OmniGraffle (see Figure 6-23):

> **The canvas**. This is where the wireframing happens.

> **The canvas list.** This allows you to add canvases and move between them. You can also add layers and move between them.

> **The Toolbar.** This provides quick access to commonly used features and tools.

> **The Inspector.** This allows you to edit various aspects of objects and canvases. Open it by selecting the Inspector button on the toolbar.

> **Stencils.** This allows you to use pre-made shapes and elements. Open it by selecting the Inspector button in the toolbar.

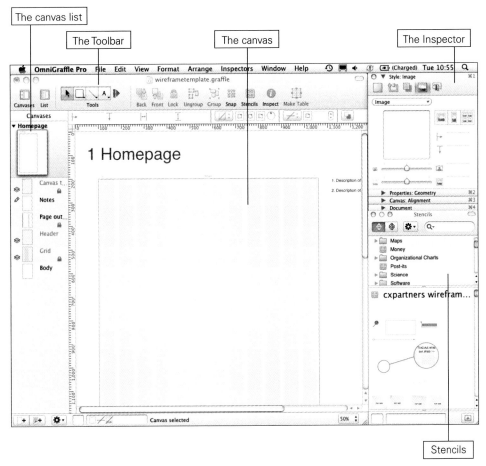

FIGURE 6-23: These are the main OmniGraffle features you will use while wireframing.

Setting up the template

This section is a step-by-step guide for creating a wireframing template in OmniGraffle. It includes dynamic page labeling, wireframe outline sizing, grid setup, and creating master objects. Although you may want your templates to look different from the one created here, going through the process will help you familiarize yourself with some of OmniGraffle's capabilities.

Creating a new document

1. Open OmniGraffle and select File, New Resource, and then New Template. A choice of templates appears.

2. Highlight the Blank template and click New Template.

Changing canvas sizing

You want to create wireframes that will scale and print well, so you need to change the page size.

1. Go to File and choose Page Setup.

2. In the page set up screen select Paper size and select Manage Custom Sizes from the list. The custom paper sizes window will appear.

3. Create a new custom size by clicking the + on the bottom left of the window. This will put a custom size called Untitled in the list.

4. Double-click the name Untitled and rename it A1. Name the custom size A1. An A1-sized page is the right scale for printing and big enough to wireframe in exact pixels.

5. Change the width to 84.1 cm and the height to 59.4 cm (see Figure 6-24).

6. Click OK and your page size should change.

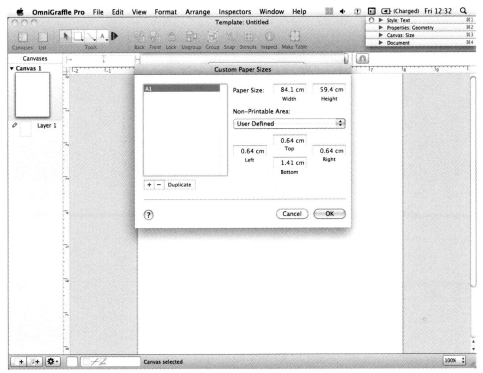

FIGURE 6-24: The sizes in this image are what you need to create an A1-sized canvas.

Changing ruler units

To change the ruler units to work in, follow these steps:

1. Open the inspector by selecting Inspectors and then choosing Show Inspectors.

2. Open the Canvas section of the inspector by clicking the arrow (see Figure 6-25). Click the Size button.

3. Change Orientation to Portrait and change Ruler units to pixels (px). As shown in Figure 6-25, the ruler scale displays across the top and down the left of your canvas changes.

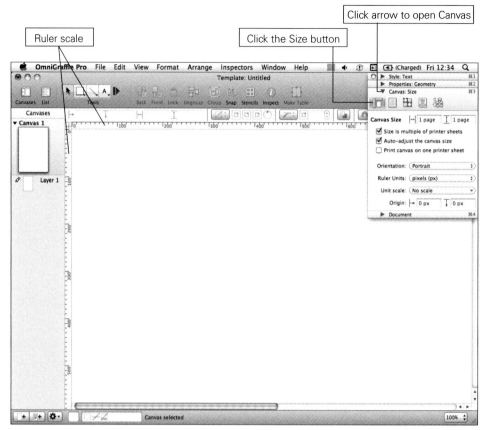

Click arrow to open Canvas

Ruler scale

Click the Size button

FIGURE 6-25: Working in actual pixels enables you to accurately measure to the site's final dimensions.

Setting up a grid

To set up a grid, follow these steps:

1. Select the Grid option from the Canvas section of the inspector.

2. Set the major grid spacing to 100 and the minor grid spacing to 10.

3. Make sure Snap to grid, Grid in front, Show grid lines, and Show major check boxes are all selected (see Figure 6-26). This will help make everything in your wireframe line up and look great.

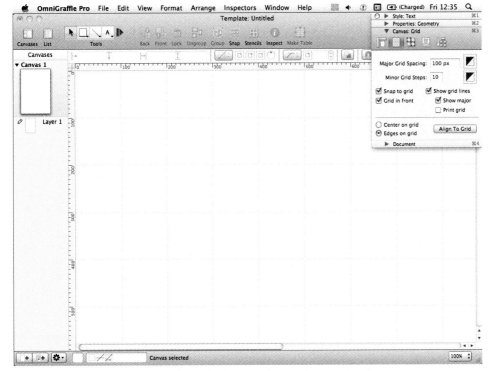

FIGURE 6-26: Working with snap to grid on makes lining up shapes and text much easier.

Creating layers

OmniGraffle allows you to work in layers, which is great. In my experience, however, it's good to keep your layers to a minimum. If you're working on a deck of wires with someone else, having too many layers can become unmanageable and selecting specific elements becomes surprisingly difficult. Here's how to create a basic layer structure.

❶ To view the layers on your canvas, click the triangle next to the canvas name. OmniGraffle starts you off with one layer, called Layer 1 by default.

❷ Edit the layer name by double-clicking it and renaming it Body. This is the layer where most of the wireframing will happen.

❸ To create a new layer either click the new layer button at the bottom of the canvas list or right-click a layer and select New Layer (see Figure 6-27).

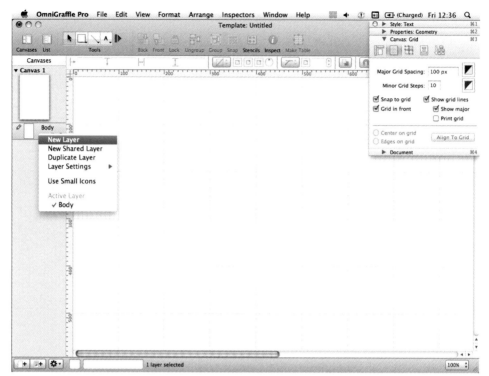

FIGURE 6-27: Right-click a layer in the canvas list to get this menu.

❹ Name your new layer Page outline. It will be the frame for your wireframe.

❺ Create one more layer and name it Notes. You'll use it for annotation.

Next you'll create shared layers.

Creating shared layers

Shared layers are really useful for areas of your wireframes that will be the same across all pages and be in the same position on all pages. It's great for things like page headers, as they remain consistent.

To create a shared layer, follow these steps:

❶ Right-click a layer and select New shared layer. A layer will appear but will be a color different than white—for example, it's turquoise (not orange) in Omnigraffle Pro 5.2.3). Name this layer Header.

❷ Repeat the process to create two more shared layers and call them Canvas title and Grid (see Figure 6-28).

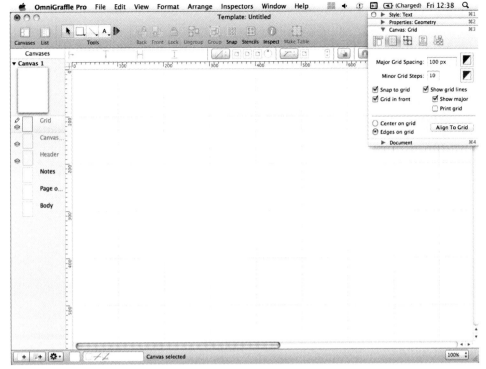

FIGURE 6-28: It's best to use as few layers as possible. Too many layers can make it difficult to tell what layer certain elements are sitting on—and that causes trouble when editing.

That should be all the layers you need for 90% of the time. However, they need to be reordered.

Reordering layers

To reorder layers, simply click and drag them. Re-order the layers like this (see Figure 6-29):

Canvas title

Notes

Page outline

Header

Body

Grid

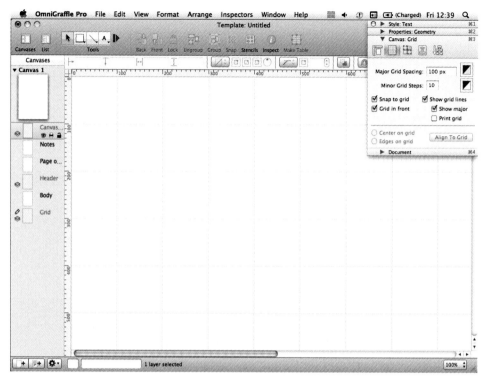

FIGURE 6-29: It's best to have the page title, outline, and notes sit above the main body of the wireframe.

Now it's time to set up the wireframe template using these layers.

note When switching between layers in OmniGraffle, simply selecting the layer you want won't work. To edit the contents of a layer you need to click to the left of the layer preview. You will know it has worked when a pencil icon appears on the layer (see Figure 6-30).

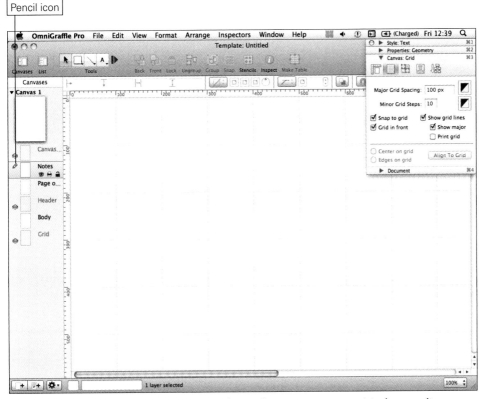

FIGURE 6-30: The Notes layer can be edited because the pencil icon appears in next to it in the canvas list.

Creating page titles with variables

OmniGraffle allows you to create dynamic page titles and numbers using variables. Variables are small bits of code that Omingaffle generates to create dynamic text boxes that automatically update to display information like page numbers or even the name of the document's author.

1 Click the Canvas title layer.

2 Click the Text tool (see Figure 6-31) and create a text box by clicking anywhere on the canvas.

Text tool

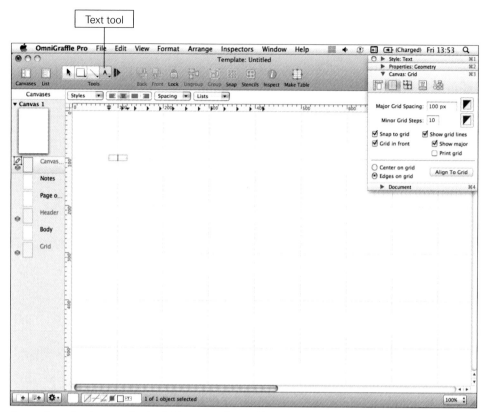

FIGURE 6-31: Creating a text box in which to insert the variable.

❸ Go to Edit, choose Variable, and then choose Page Number. The text box will be filled with some odd-looking symbols (see Figure 6-32).

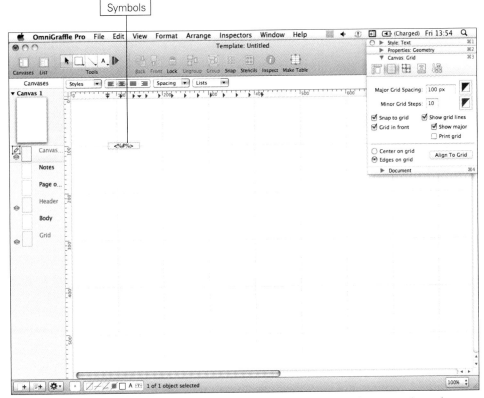

FIGURE 6-32: The odd-looking symbols are the code that the variable uses to pull in the page number to the text box.

4 Click outside of the text box and it should change to a number 1. This means it's figuring out the page number and displaying it, so you don't have to.

5 To add a page title, click in the text box and add a space after the page number variable.

6 Go to Edit, choose Insert Variable, and then choose Canvas Name.

7 Click out of the text box. It should now read 1 Canvas 1 (see Figure 6-33). It's getting the name from the canvas list on the left.

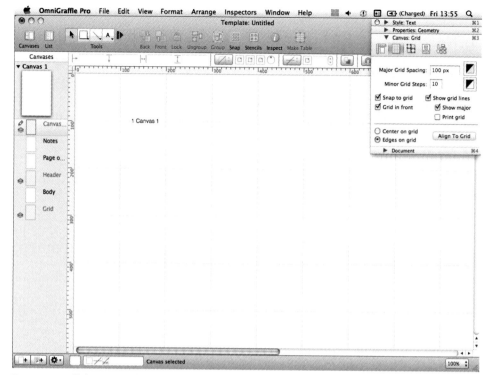

FIGURE 6-33: Clicking out of the text box will show the variable working and displaying the page number.

8 To change the page name, double-click the name of the canvas in the list on the left, change the name to Homepage, and then press Enter. The text box on the canvas should now read 1 Homepage (see Figure 6-34).

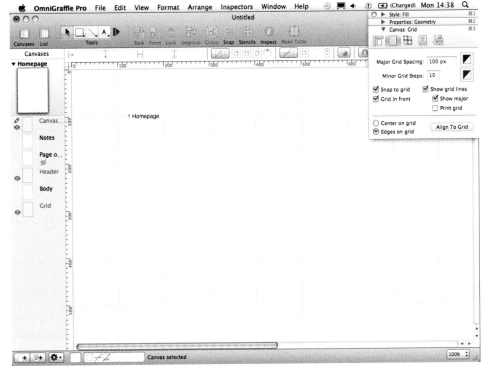

FIGURE 6-34: The variables in the text box are now displaying the canvas number and the canvas name specified in the canvas list.

❾ To change the style of the page title, open the Style panel of the inspector and click the Text button (see Figure 6-35). From here you can edit the color size and font type.

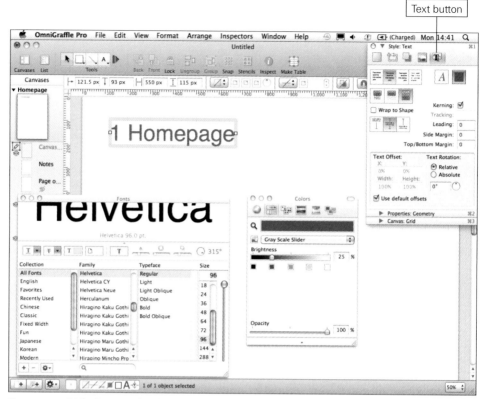

Text button

FIGURE 6-35: Make the page title and number large.

Working with the page outline

In this section, you'll learn how to work with the page outline, including how to:

> Create shapes

> Set sizes

> Set positions

> Set styles

Begin by creating a shape:

❶ Select the Page outline layer, being sure that the pencil icon appears on the layer in the canvas list.

❷ Select the shape tool from the tool palette and draw a rectangle of any size (see Figure 6-36). In this example, the size is 230 px wide by 140 px high.

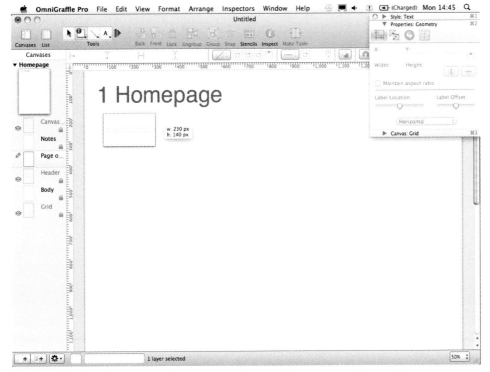

FIGURE 6-36: It doesn't matter what size rectangle you draw; you'll change its size in the next step.

❸ Open the Properties panel in the inspector and click the Geometry button. From here, you can accurately set the size and position of the rectangle:

1. Set the x position to 100 px and the y to 200 px to give the rectangle enough border and space for the page title.

2. Set the rectangle width to 960 px.

3. Set the height to 2000 (see Figure 6-37). This will fit the canvas but the length of the page outline is likely to be different on every page (that is why you don't use a shared layer).

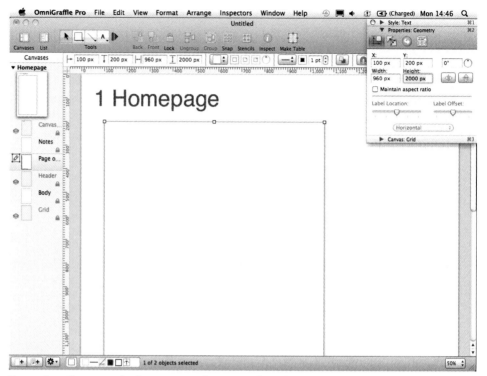

FIGURE 6-37: You can use the Geometry controls to accurately set the size and position of a shape.

Finally, you need to remove some of the styles from the outline:

1. Remove the shadow by selecting the outline, opening the Style panel of the inspector, and selecting the Shadow option. Deselect the shadow check box.

2. Remove the fill by selecting the Fill option and deselecting the Fill checkbox.

3. Change the line style by selecting the Lines and Shapes option and changing the line color to a medium gray (see Figure 6-38). (You want the outline to frame the wireframe, not take attention away from it.)

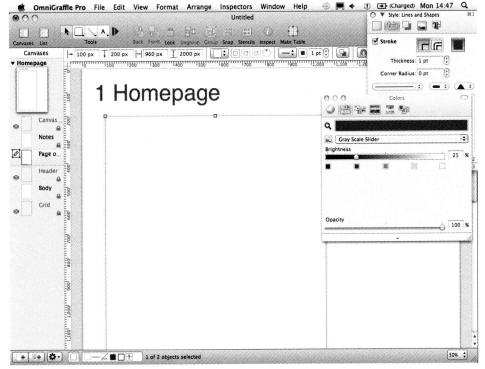

FIGURE 6-38: A light outline for your wireframe will show where the wireframe starts and stops but not take attention away from it.

Creating a custom page grid

In this section, you'll learn how to use shapes and layers to create a custom grid to design with, including:

> Duplicating an object

> Spacing an object

> Changing a line style

You'll begin by duplicating an object:

1 Draw another rectangle using the shape tool, only this time use the Style panel in the inspector.

2 Remove the shadow and the stroke.

3 Set the color to red and set the opacity to 10% (see Figure 6-39).

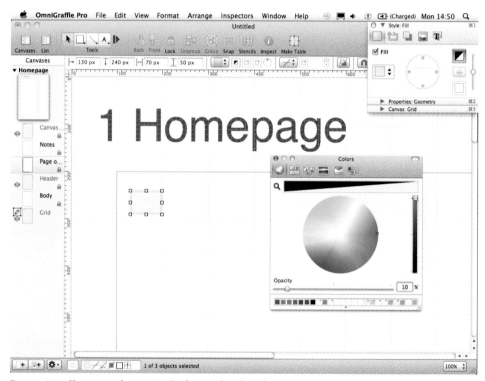

FIGURE 6-39: You can set the opacity of a shape within the Colors menu.

4 Click the Properties: Geometry down-arrow (see Figure 6-40) and change the Width of the rectangle to 60 px and the Height to 2000 px.

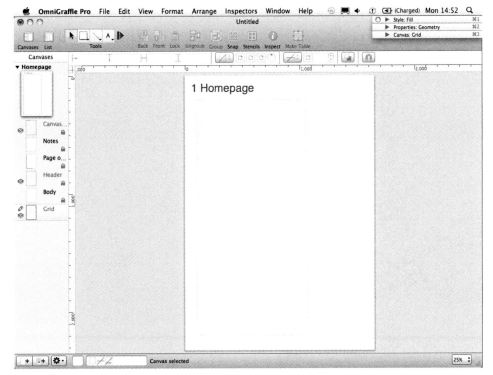

FIGURE 6-40: Make sure the rectangle runs from the top of the page outline to the bottom.

5 Place the rectangle at the top of the wireframe so it runs from the top of the wireframe's outline to the bottom. Move it so it's 10 pixels from the left edge of the wireframe outline. Make sure Snap to grid is turned on so it can be easily dragged into position.

Now you need to duplicate the rectangle:

1 Select the rectangle and press Cmd+D to duplicate.

2 Place the new rectangle 20 pixels to the right of the original, making sure it's aligned to the top of the wireframe outline (see Figure 6-41).

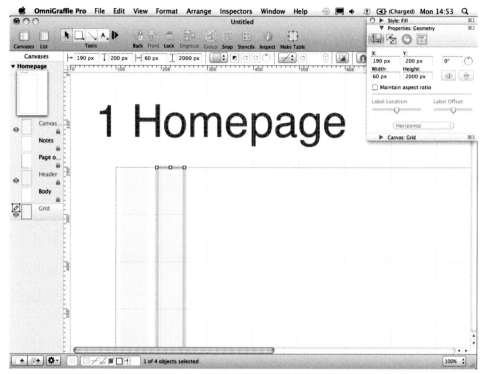

FIGURE 6-41: The first rectangle should be 10 pixels from the side of the page outline. Then leave a 20-pixel space between each rectangle.

❸ With the duplicate rectangle still selected, press Cmd+D again to repeat the process.

tip When you duplicate objects, OmniGraffle remembers the relative positions of the original object and its duplicate. So if you duplicate again, all objects will be equally spaced apart.

❹ Keep duplicating the rectangle, spacing them 20 pixels apart, until you have 12 rectangles with 20-pixel gutters between each and 10-pixel buffers on the left and right edges of the wireframe (see Figure 6-42).

The final part of creating the grid is to label its dimensions. This provides the design and development team a clear idea of page widths and grid sizes. Follow these steps:

❶ Select the line tool and draw a line 10 pixels above the wireframe outline that runs from the left edge of the first rectangle to the right edge of the last rectangle (see Figure 6-43).

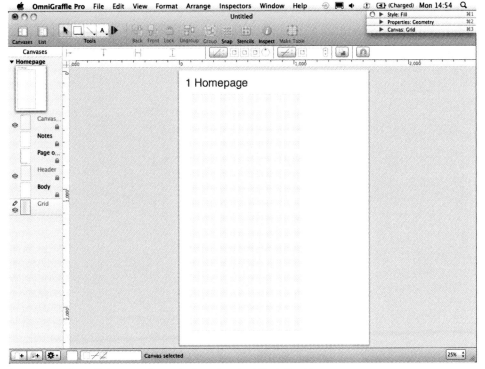

FIGURE 6-42: Once all the rectangles are in place, they should look like this.

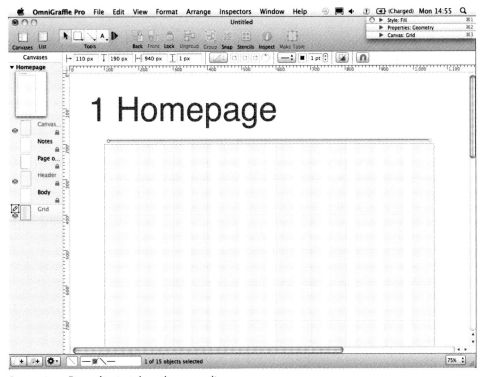

FIGURE 6-43: Draw a line just above the page outline.

❷ Click the Style drop-down in the inspector to open the Style panel.

❸ Click the Line arrow style drop-down to change the stroke end and start points to arrows.

❹ Change the stroke color to a medium gray (see Figure 6-44).

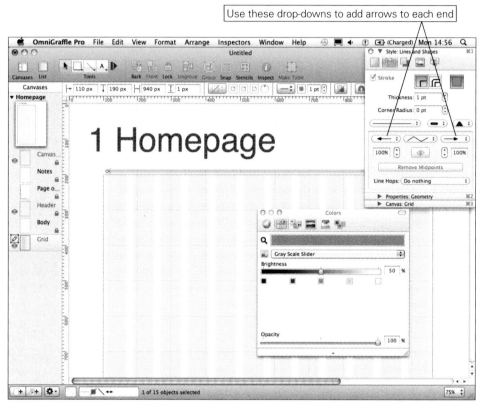

FIGURE 6-44: Change the line color to light grey and add arrows to each end.

❺ Create a text box and type 960.

❻ Set the background color of the text box to white and the font color to the same medium gray (see Figure 6-45).

❼ Use the text options in the Style part of the inspector to center the text box on the line (see Figure 6-48).

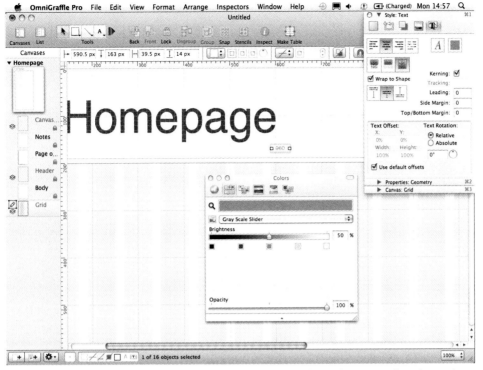

FIGURE 6-45: Adding the dimensions helps the designers and developers know what size templates they need to work to.

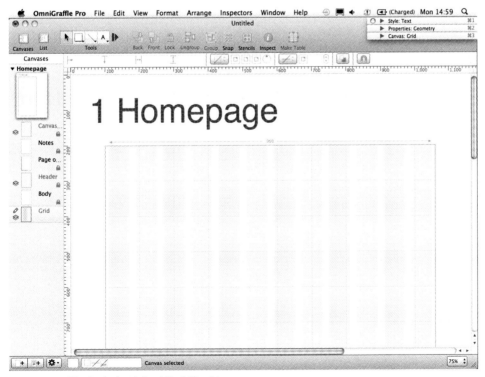

FIGURE 6-46: The finished grid should look like this.

Creating LinkBack objects

LinkBack is a technique that allows you to create master objects that work in a way that is similar to shared layers. If you create duplicates of a LinkBack object and edit one of them, all the duplicated objects will update and match each other. This is really useful for areas like footers because they need to look the same on all pages but need to be on different positions on the page.

To create a LinkBack object, follow these steps:

1 Select the Body layer.

2 Create a rectangle for the footer. Color, style it, and add some text (see Figure 6-47).

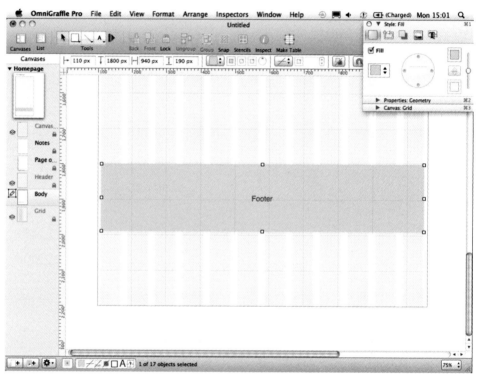

FIGURE 6-47: Create a simple footer element to turn into a master object.

3 Right-click the rectangle, click Copy As, and then choose PDF (see Figure 6-48).

4 Delete the rectangle and then paste it back onto the canvas. You have now created the LinkBack object.

5 To demonstrate how it works, duplicate the object by pressing Cmd+D, so you now have two rectangles (see Figure 6-49).

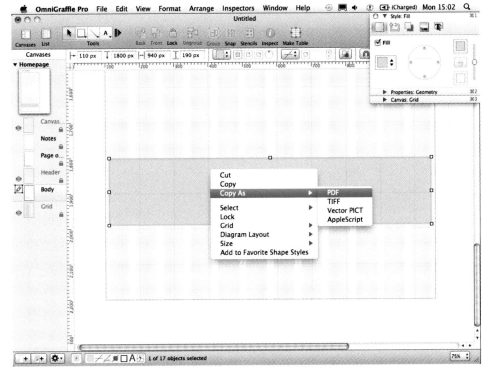

FIGURE 6-48: Copying as a PDF file.

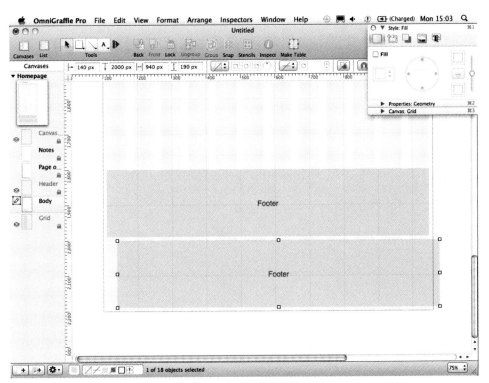

FIGURE 6-49: When you paste the object back onto the canvas, it will be a LinkBack master object.

❻ Double-click the rectangle to edit it. A new window displays with your rectangle in it. Notice the file name starts with LinkBack.

❼ Now edit your LinkBack file. The file shown in Figure 6-50 looks more like a footer.

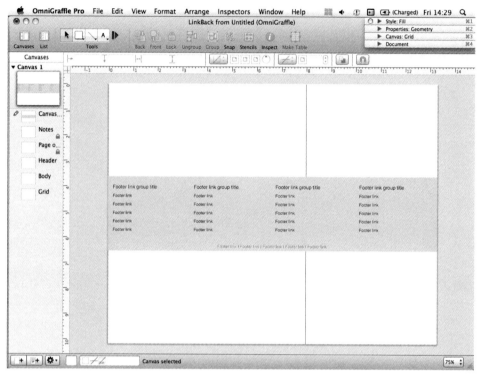

FIGURE 6-50: When you double-click your master object, a new canvas opens it for editing.

❽ Go to File and choose Save (or use the keyboard shortcut Cmd+S).

❾ Close the Linkback window.

Both rectangles on your template are updated and they should be identical (see Figure 6-51).

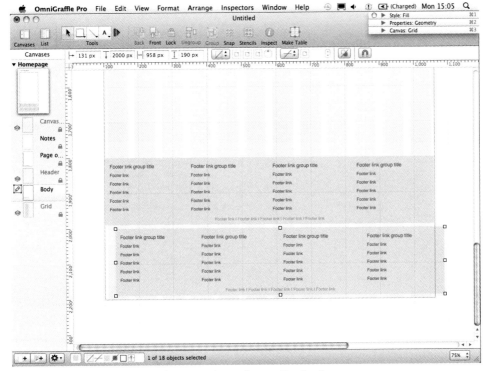

FIGURE 6-51: When you edit one of the master objects, they are all updated.

Creating the wireframes

This section explains how to use OmniGraffle to create common elements found in wireframes, including text, lists, image masks, and button styles. You'll put it all together to create a wireframe for a hotel details page for a travel website.

Using basic boxes to mark out content areas

Begin the wireframe by marking out all the content areas with simple boxes. To create visual heat and make the content areas and the header stand out, you will use a gray background and white content panels.

❶ To create the background, make sure you are working in the Body layer of your document.

❷ Select the rectangle from the shape tool and draw a box.

❸ In the Style section of the inspector panel, change the Fill color to 85% gray and remove the Stroke and Shadow.

❹ Resize the box to cover the entire wire frame, but leaving space at the top for the header (see Figure 6-52).

❺ Once your background is in place, select it and click the lock option in the tool bar. This prevents you from moving your background by accident.

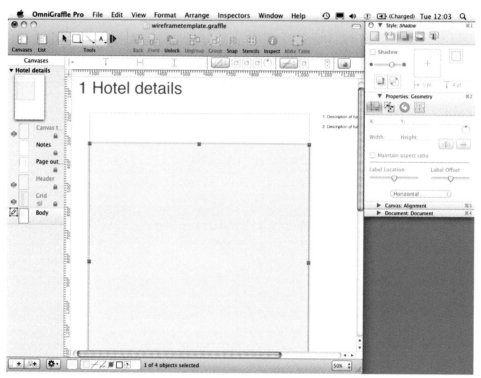

FIGURE 6-52: Make sure the background rectangle is locked so it doesn't get moved accidentally.

Now create more boxes, but this time, make them white and remove shadows and lines. Use the grid you created to lay out your content areas. This page will hold the main hotel details area., a booking form area, a promo area, and a cross-sell area across the bottom of the page (see Figure 6-53).

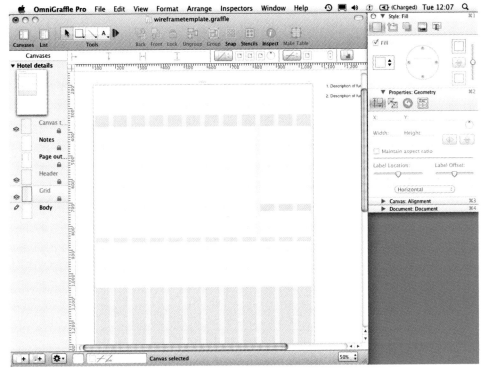

FIGURE 6-53: The custom grid helps to lay out the content areas.

If you created a footer object during the template setup, put it in as well.

Using image placeholders

Using images in wireframes is not always practical or possible. Instead, use a placeholder whereby images are represented by a box filled with an X.

To create image placeholders, follow these steps:

❶ Select the rectangle from the shape tool and draw a box.

❷ In the Style section of the inspector panel, change the Fill color to 75% gray and remove the Stroke and Shadow (see Figure 6-54).

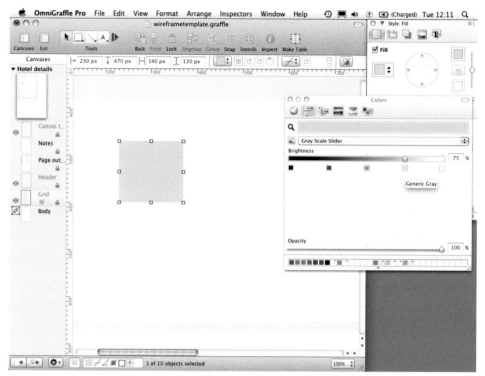

FIGURE 6-54: Make sure the stroke and shadow are removed from the rectangle.

❸ Select the line tool (making sure you have the straight line selected) and draw a line from one corner of the box to the opposite corner. You'll notice this doesn't work. That's because the line is magnetic.

OmniGraffle makes magnetic lines stick to objects at predefined points, which is really useful for creating sitemaps, but not so useful for wireframing.

❹ To stop this from happening, draw a line wherever you can.

❺ With the line selected, click the Magnet button (see Figure 6-55) in the top menu. The magnet button should show a red line through it and the ends of your line should turn blue.

> **note** If you cannot see the magnet option it's probably because you have rulers turned off. To turn them on from the top menu, click View and then choose Rulers.

❻ Position your non-magnetic line so it runs from one corner of your box diagonally to the opposite corner,

❼ In the Style section of the inspector, change the line color to 40% gray, the thickness to 0.5 and change the stroke to a dashed line (see Figure 6-56).

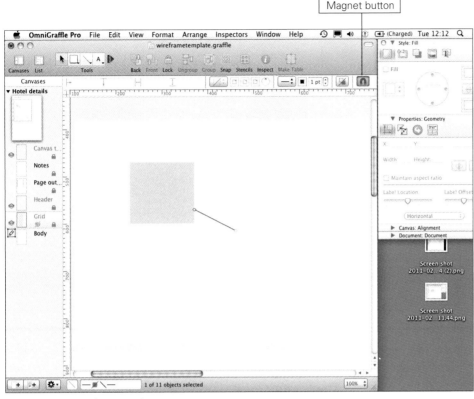

FIGURE 6-55: Using the Magnet button.

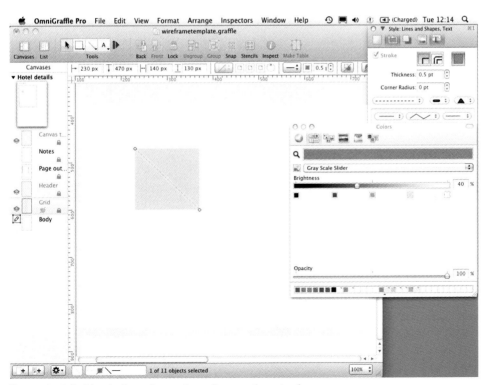

FIGURE 6-56: Position the line so it runs diagonally across the rectangle.

8 Duplicate the line (Cmd+D) and position it so it runs diagonally across the box in the opposite direction (see Figure 6-57).

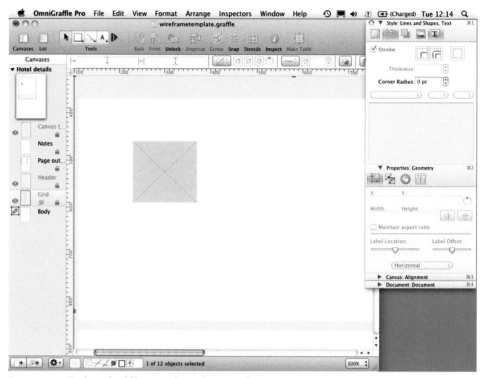

FIGURE 6-57: The lines should be crossed over the rectangle.

9 Group the box and lines using the Group button in the toolbar (or use the keyboard shortcut Shift+Cmd+G).

Lastly you need to add a label to your image. It will describe the type of image that's intended to be placed on the page.

10 Use the text tool to create a text box and type your label. Call it Hotel image.

11 Center your text box on your image placeholder using the alignment part of the canvas panel in the inspector.

12 In the Style panel of the inspector, include a fill in your text box and make the fill color match the image placeholders. This stops the lines and the text from interfering with each other.

13 Change the text color to a 40% gray (see Figure 6-58). The label needs to be subtle and not have the same weight as body copy or headers.

14 Finally, use the Group button to group all the elements together. You have your image placeholder!

Now you'll add these placeholders to the cross promotions panel. Use the grid you created to make sure they are spaced evenly (see Figure 6-59).

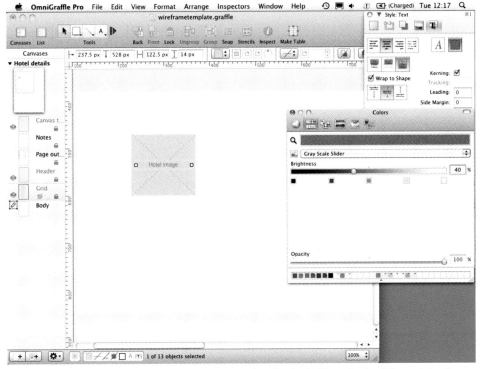

FIGURE 6-58: The image placeholder text should be centered on the placeholder and it should be a subtle color.

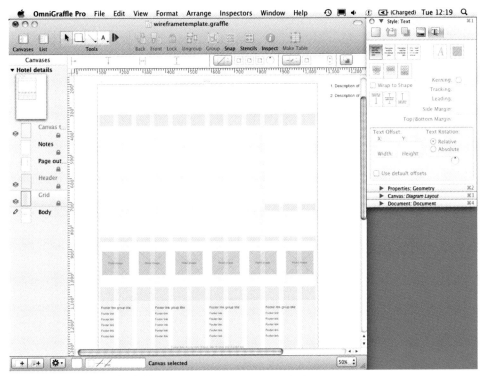

FIGURE 6-59: Use image placeholders to represent images on your wireframe.

Creating tabs

In this section, you'll learn how to create tabs and how to create custom tab shapes.

To create a tab, follow these steps:

❶ Select the rectangle from the shape tool and draw a box for your tab. Make it 20 pixels taller than you want it to end up being. We are going to remove some of it later.

❷ Use the Style panel of the inspector to change the color of your tab.

❸ In the Lines and Shapes section of the Style panel, remove the stroke and set the Corner Radius to 10 (see Figure 6-60). This gives you the nice rounded tab look, but you don't want rounded corners on the bottom.

❹ Draw another box over your tab so it covers the rounded corners at the bottom (see Figure 6-61).

❺ Select the tab and the box on top of it. Go go Edit, choose Shapes, and then choose Subtract Shapes (see Figure 6-62).

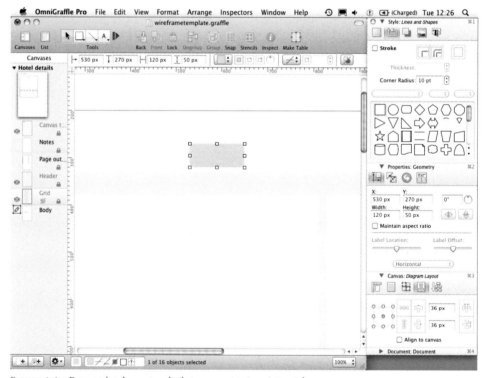

FIGURE 6-60: Draw and style a rectangle that you want to turn into a tab.

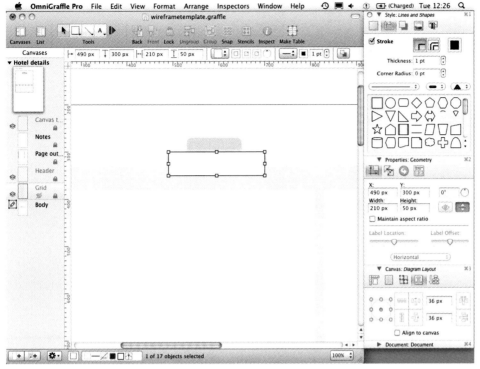

FIGURE 6-61: Place another rectangle over the part of the rectangle underneath that you want to remove.

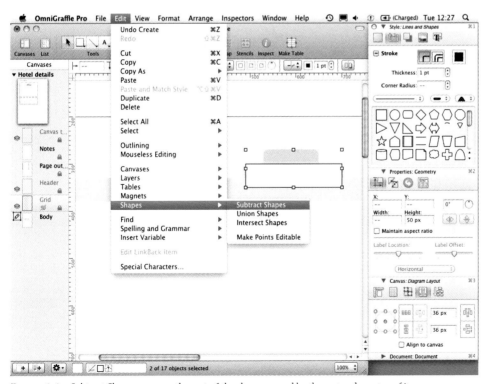

FIGURE 6-62: Subtract Shapes removes the part of the shape covered by the rectangle on top of it.

This will use the top rectangle as a guide to delete a portion of whatever is selected below it. You now have a tab with rounded top corners and a straight bottom edge (see Figure 6-63).

6 Duplicate this shape to make as many tabs as you need.

7 Color the selected tab the same as the main background color.

8 Make all of the unselected tabs darker (see Figure 6-64).

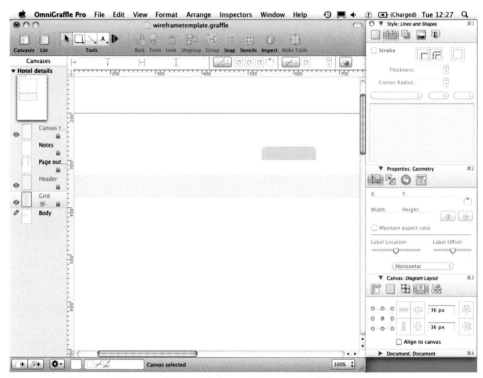

FIGURE 6-63: Removing the bottom of the rounded rectangle creates the tab shape.

Alternatively you can create custom shapes by combining objects. Here's how to create a different tab style that you'll use for the in-page navigation:

1 Create boxes for your tabs (see Figure 6-65). Style them how you want.

2 To create the selected tab, pick the one you want to be selected and duplicate it.

3 With the duplicate selected, open the Lines and Shapes section of the Style panel in the inspector. Several shapes are displayed in this panel; simply click the shape you want. This example uses the downward facing triangle (see Figure 6-66).

4 Position the triangle over the tab you want to use, go to Edit, click Shapes, and then choose Union Shapes (see Figure 6-67).

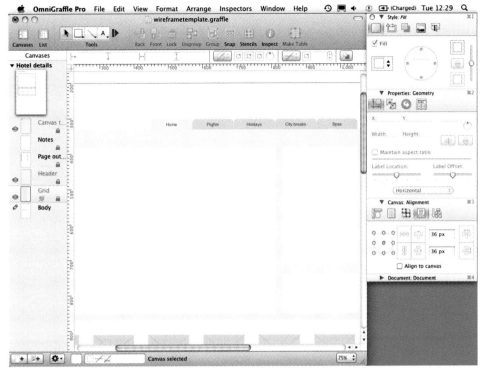

FIGURE 6-64: You can use these tab shapes to create top navigation.

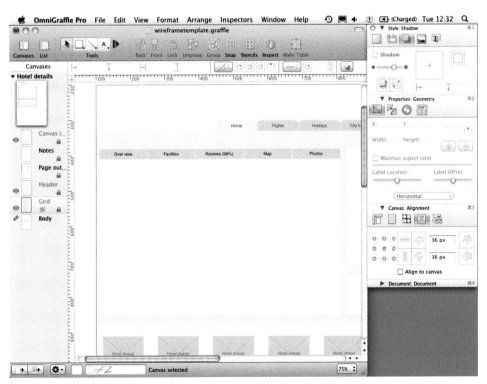

FIGURE 6-65: Create all the rectangles for your tabs in page navigation.

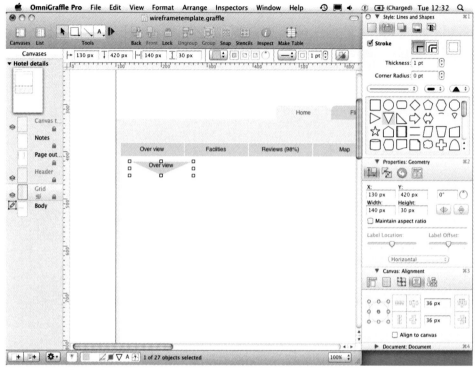

FIGURE 6-66: Change the shape to a downward triangle.

FIGURE 6-67: Union Shapes turns the rectangle and triangle into a single custom shape.

These two shapes will become one, but the text will look out of alignment. To fix that:

5 Open the Text part of the Style panel in the inspector.

6 Set the vertical alignment to Top and change the Top/Bottom Margin to 10 (see Figure 6-68).

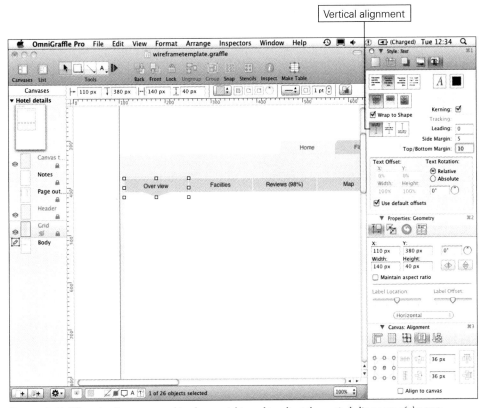

FIGURE 6-68: When the shapes are combined, you might need to adjust the vertical alignment of the text.

Adding images

Sometimes you will need to use images in your wireframes. There are a couple of things worth remembering about OmniGraffle and images.

OmniGraffle won't let you drag images straight from a web browser. Instead you need to drag images from the browser to your desktop, then you must drag the images from your desktop into OmniGraffle.

OmniGraffle doesn't grayscale images. When using images in wireframes, it's good practice to remove all color from them. Having colored images gives them an unfair advantage in testing because everything else is grayscale. You will need to grayscale your images outside of OmniGraffle. The image viewing application Preview can achieve this easily. You should find it in the applications folder on your Mac; it comes as part of the operating system.

There are two useful ways that OmniGraffle allows you to edit images:

> The Stretch to fit button, which is located in the Image section of the Style part of the inspector. It allows you to resize the image in the same way you would any object or shape.

> The Natural size button allows you to specify an area of the image to mask and allows you to resize the image within this area.

OmniGraffle uses Stretch to fit by default, so use that for the main hotel image.

❶ Drag an image onto the canvas and resize it to be your main image (see Figure 6-69).

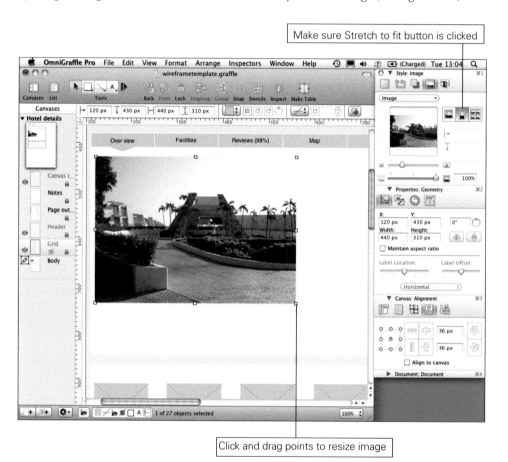

FIGURE 6-69: Resize the image by selecting it and dragging any of the points.

For the thumbnails image, use the Natural size button. This is the way OmniGraffle masks images.

② To use natural size, drag an image onto your canvas.

③ Select the image and open the Style panel of the inspector.

④ Select the images section. You will see three different icons of mountains. These allow you to switch between Stretch to fit, Natural size, and Tile.

⑤ Select the left icon for Natural size.

If you try to resize your image on the canvas, you will see that the image doesn't change size; instead it becomes masked. This is really useful if you only want a portion of the image visible.

⑥ Set the mask area so the image is a small thumbnail under the main hotel image (see Figure 6-70).

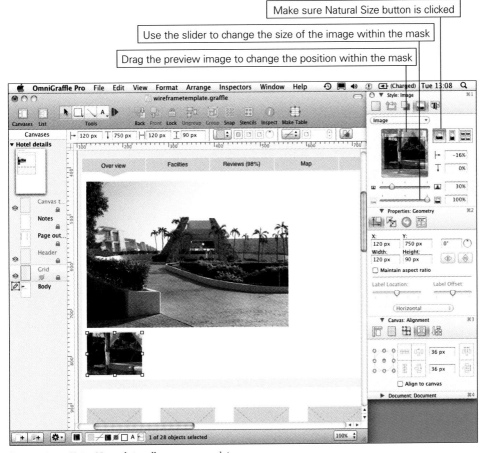

FIGURE 6-70: Using Natural size allows you to mask images.

❼ To resize the image, use the size slider on the image section of the style panel in the inspector (see Figure 6-71). You can also adjust the position of the image within the mask by dragging the image in the position box on the inspector.

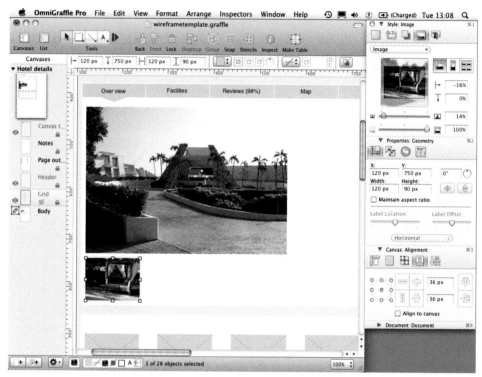

FIGURE 6-71: Natural size allows you to use masks that allow you to make the image fill any size or shape you set.

Getting your mask right can be tricky, but this method is really useful if you want multiple images to be the same size.

❽ Duplicate the masked image and drag a new image into OmniGraffle directly onto your duplicated image. (You should see a blue outline appear.)

❾ Drop the new image over the duplicated one; it will replace it with the same mask applied (see Figure 6-72).

FIGURE 6-72: Dragging a new image over a Natural size image will create a blue highlight.

Adding text

In this section, you'll learn how to create and manipulate text, including how to add bulleted lists and how to set line spacing.

To add text, follow these steps:

1 Select the text tool and create a new text box for the page header.

2 Type the page title (for example, Sirens Hotel Mexico).

3 Using the Text part of the Style panel in the inspector, set the text alignment to left.

4 Change the font size by clicking the A button, which opens the Fonts dialog (see Figure 6-73).

5 Change the color of the text to 10% black. Avoid using a pure black font, which makes the text look "harsh." Your page will look cluttered.

6 Create another text box next to the hotel image. Give it a heading (about 18 pt), some body copy (12 pt), and a list (see Figure 6-74).

FIGURE 6-73: Clicking the A button in the Style: Text section of the inspector opens this font popup.

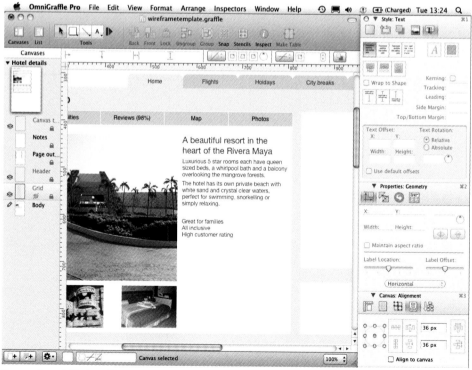

FIGURE 6-74: Add a list of 3 or more items.

❼ Double-click into the text box.

Notice the options above the ruler units at the top of the page have changed. The two you are going to use are Spacing and Lists. You'll use these to turn the short list into a bulleted list.

❽ Highlight the text you want to add bullet points to, click the Lists down-arrow, and then choose the round text bullet option.

Each line should have a bullet next to it. If the indent of the bullet points and the text is not quite right, you can adjust it using the arrows on the ruler units at the top of the canvas. Make sure all the text you want to adjust is selected (see Figure 6-75).

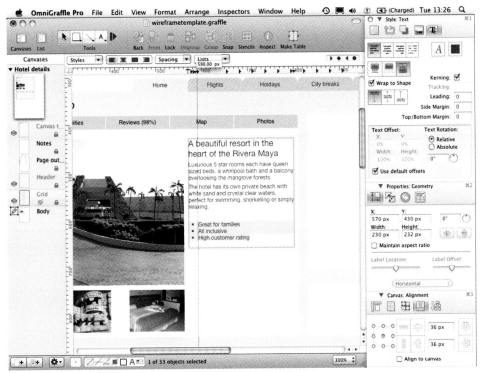

FIGURE 6-75: Once the bullet points are added, you can drag the arrows in the rulers above the canvas to adjust the text and bullet indents.

❾ To create more space between each item in the list, making it easier to read, highlight all the text.

❿ Click the Spacing drop-down and choose Other.

⓫ Change Paragraph spacing after to 10.0 points (see Figure 6-76).

FIGURE 6-76: Change the Paragraph spacing after so the position of the top of the list is not affected.

Creating buttons

Buttons and calls to action are key elements of a web page, especially in product pages. It's important that buttons look like actual buttons in wireframes so they're clearly understood by stakeholders and users during testing. Here's how to make them in OmniGraffle:

❶ Select the rectangle from the shape tool and draw a box for your button.

❷ In the Style panel in the inspector, select the Fill check box.

❸ Change the Fill type to Double Linear Blend (see Figure 6-77). Three color boxes and a vertical slider appear (see Figure 6-78).

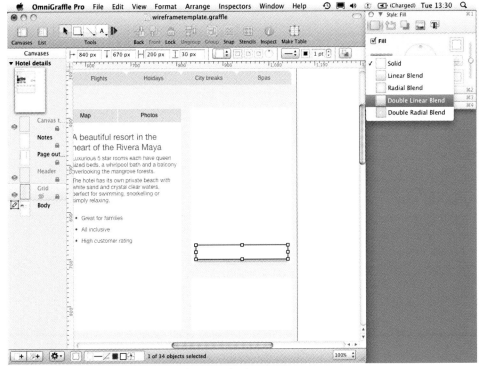

FIGURE 6-77: Change the Fill type to Double Linear Blend.

Adjust all the colors in the blend to create a bevelled effect.

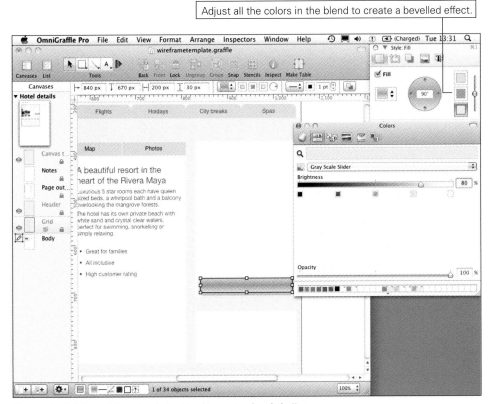

FIGURE 6-78: Adjust all the colors in the blend to create a beveled effect.

④ Change the top color to a light 75% gray.

⑤ Change the middle color to a darker 50% gray.

⑥ Change the bottom color to a lighter 80% gray.

The button is starting to look beveled but needs some tweaking.

⑦ Use the vertical slider to change the position of your gradient and bring it down so the lightest gray shows only at the bottom of the button (see Figure 6-79).

Drag the slider to adjust the postion of the gradient

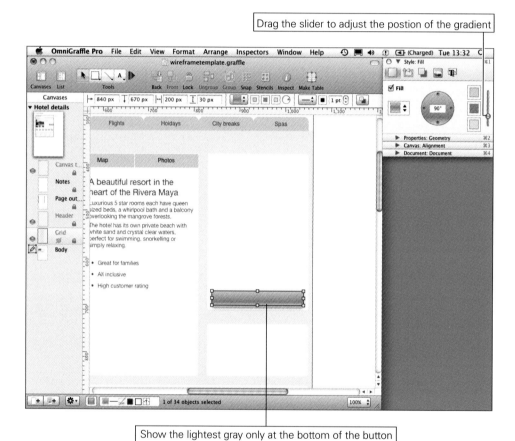

Show the lightest gray only at the bottom of the button

FIGURE 6-79: Adjust the position of the gradient.

The default line style and shadow styles look pretty awful, so you'll want to change those, too.

❽ In the Lines and Shapes section of the Style panel, change the stroke color to a 50% gray. This makes the button stand out against the background without being too harsh.

❾ Set the Corner Radius to five to give the button rounded edges (see Figure 6-80).

❿ Switch to the Shadow section to edit the various aspects of the shadows.

⓫ Use the slider to change the amount the shadow is blurred.

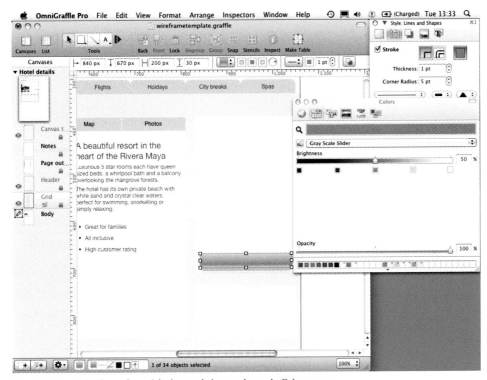

FIGURE 6-80: Make the outline of the button lighter and round off the corners.

You can toggle between showing the shadow immediately below the button or below every other object.

To change the position of the shadow, click within the shadow position box. You can be more accurate by adding vertical and horizontal values below. To move the shadow up or right, you need to use negative numbers.

You can adjust the color and opacity of your shadow (see Figure 6-81). It's a good idea not to make the shadow too dark because it can make the button look messy.

⓬ Add some text to your button.

That finishes the button. You can use the gradient technique used to create this button to create affordance on other interface elements, like drop-downs and check boxes (see Figure 6-82).

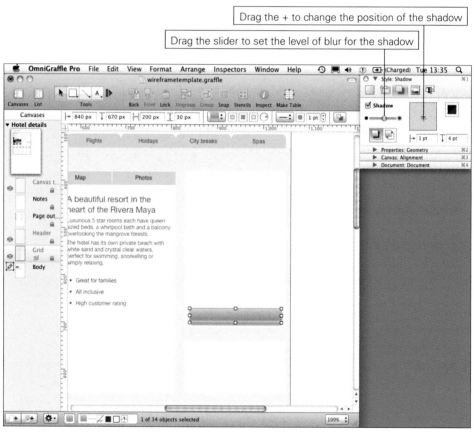

FIGURE 6-81: Shadow will add affordance to your button.

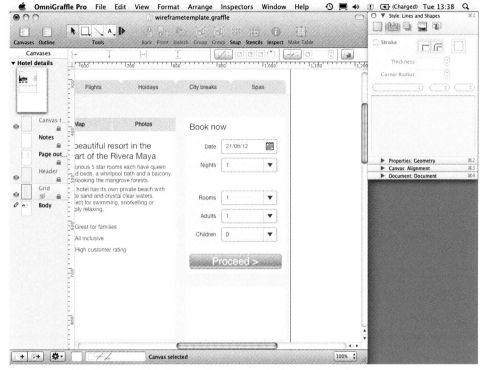

FIGURE 6-82: Affordance is useful for buttons, drop-downs and other wireframe elements.

Using stencils

Stencils are a great way to speed up your workflow. They allow you to save specific elements that you have created to easily use in later projects. There are also a ton of great stencils already out there for you to download and use (including one created for this book).

To use a stencil, follow these steps:

❶ Click the Stencils button on the toolbar.

A panel displays with a list of default stencil sets for you to use.

❷ Select a stencil set and the contents of the stencil will appear (see Figure 6-83).

FIGURE 6-83: Using stencils.

❸ Drag the element you want to use onto the page.

To create a new stencil, follow these steps:

❶ Go to File, click New Resource, and then choose New Stencil.

❷ Put all the elements you want for your stencil onto the canvas and save it. It now appears in your stencils panel (see Figure 6-84).

tip Remember to group all the shapes that make up your element. You can only drag individual objects from stencils onto your canvas.

To edit your stencil, right-click the stencil in the stencils palette and select Edit stencil.

To use downloaded stencils, put the stencil in the right folder in your library by going to Library, clicking Application Support, choosing OmniGraffle, and then choosing Stencils.

So that's all you need to get you started making wireframes. You can use all you have learned here to finish off your hotel details page by adding the remaining headings labels and icons shown in Figure 6-85.

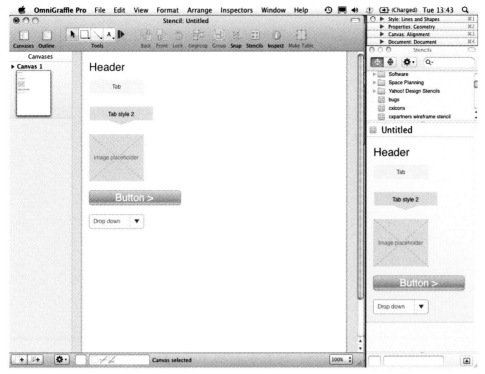

FIGURE 6-84: Any changes you make to the stencil while editing will automatically update in the stencil window.

FIGURE 6-85: The finished wireframe will look like this.

HOW TO Create wireframes in Axure

Axure is a fantastic tool for creating interactive prototypes. But before you make anything interactive you need to create a well thought out set of wireframes. This section shows you some basic techniques for creating wireframe elements in Axure. First, however, you need to become more familiar with Axure.

An overview of Axure

Figure 6-86 shows the basic layout of the Axure window, including:

> **Toolbar.** This allows you to format the color and style of objects and text.

> **Sitemap pane.** This is where you navigate between the pages you are editing.

> **Widgets pane.** This stores all the useful that you can use to start building your wireframe.

> **Masters pane.** This stores all the custom widgets that you create.

> **Canvas.** This is where the wireframing happens.

> **Widget Properties pane.** This is where you can add notes and interactions and format the size and position of objects.

Toolbar   Sitemap pane

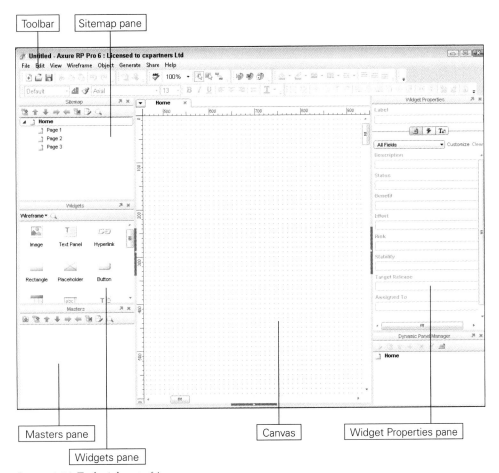

Masters pane   Canvas   Widget Properties pane

Widgets pane

FIGURE 6-86: The basic layout of Axure.

Creating wireframes

In this section, you'll learn how to create and style basic shapes, edit text and bullets, add images, create custom buttons, and create master objects.

Creating and styling basic shapes

To create a shape, follow these steps:

1. Drag a Rectangle from the widgets pane onto the canvas. There are several other basic shapes in the library if you need them.

2. Select the Rectangle on the canvas. You can position and resize your object by dragging, but for more accuracy, you can use the Location and Size pane on the bottom right (see Figure 6-87).

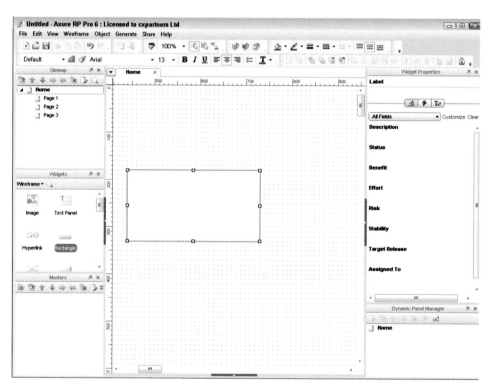

FIGURE 6-87: To create a rectangle, drag one from the widgets pane onto the canvas.

You can use the toolbar to change font styles and alignment and the shape color and line style.

To change the fill color, select the shape and click the Fill Color drop-down (see Figure 6-88). From here you can select from a pre-defined set of colors.

tip You can click More to get a more detailed color palette, or use the color picker to copy a color from anywhere on the screen.

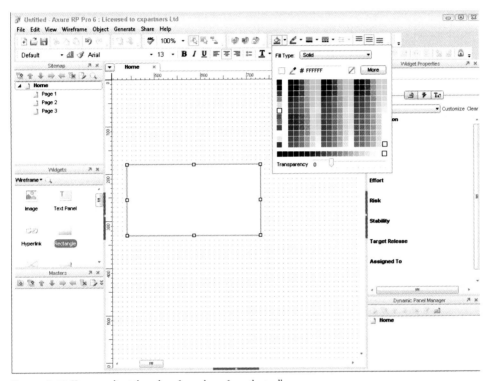

FIGURE 6-88: You can adjust the color of any shape from the toolbar.

The Fill icon changes to match the color you picked. This is because the color drop-down remembers the last color you selected, which makes it easy to make multiple objects the same color. To do this, select the shape you want to color and click the Fill icon (*not* the Fill drop-down arrow).

Change the line color the same way. The drop-down to the right allows you to change line weight or remove it completely. The drop-down to the right of that allows you to change the line style (see Figure 6-89).

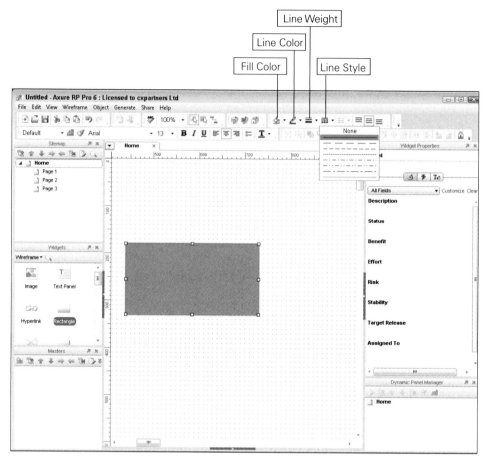

FIGURE 6-89: Adjusting line styles.

Editing text and bullets

Editing text in Axure is fairly limited. You can do the basics like changing font style size and color, but indenting and line spacing are not available. In this section, you'll learn how to create a basic header, how to create body copy, and how to create a bulleted list, and you'll learn a workaround for line spacing.

To create a basic header, follow these steps:

❶ Drag a Text Panel from the widgets library pane onto your canvas.

❷ Double-click it to edit the text and add your heading.

❸ With the text panel selected, go to toolbar and change the font size to 18 and change the color to a dark gray (see Figure 6-90). It's a good idea not to use 100% black in your wireframes because it makes the page look cluttered.

To create body copy, follow Steps 1–3 but use a smaller font (see Figure 6-91).

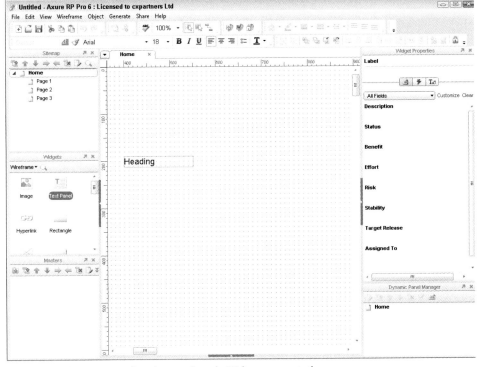

FIGURE 6-90: To create a text box, drag one from the Widgets pane onto the canvas.

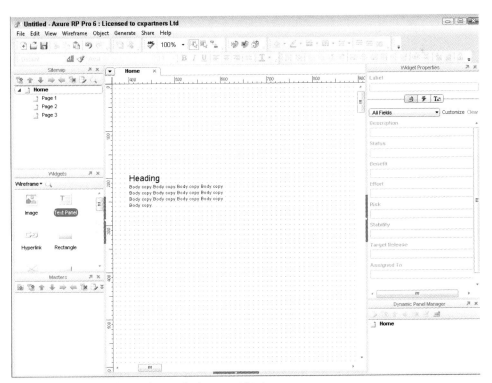

FIGURE 6-91: Double click a text box to edit the copy within it.

When creating bulleted lists, it's a good idea to create a separate text panel from your body copy (see Figure 6-92). This allows you to indent the text by moving the text panel.

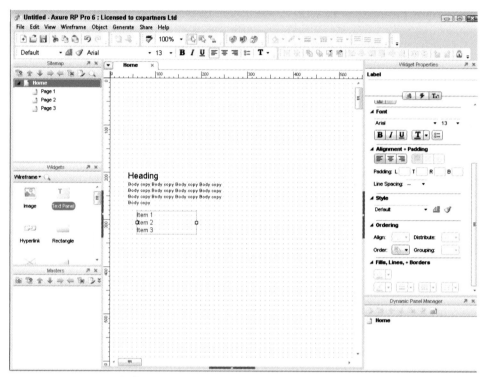

FIGURE 6-92: Putting your bulleted lists in a separate text box allows you to indent the bullets more easily against the rest of the text.

➊ Create the list you want.

➋ Select all the text you want to include in the bulleted list and select the bullets button in the toolbar.

➌ To change the line spacing, select all the text in the bulleted list and open the Formatting section of the Widgets Properties pane (see Figure 6-93). Use the Line Spacing drop-down to set the line spacing to 24.

Click to open the Formatting section

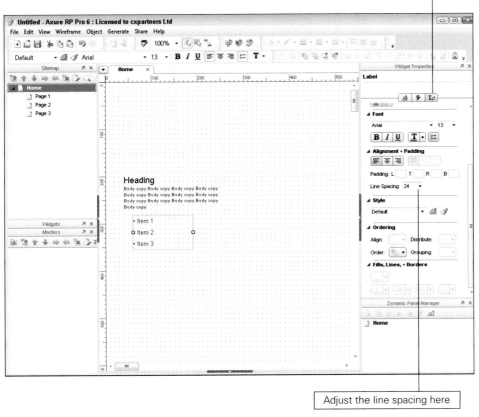

Adjust the line spacing here

FIGURE 6-93: Setting line spacing from the Widgets properties pane.

Adding images

Axure has very little control over images, so it's a good idea to prep them before adding them to your wireframe. Get the right crop and grayscale them if necessary.

To add an image:

❶ Drag an Image object from the widgets pane onto your wireframe (see Figure 6-94).

❷ Position it and resize it to where you want your image to be.

❸ Right-click the Image object and select Edit Image > Import Image.

❹ Select the image you want and click Open.

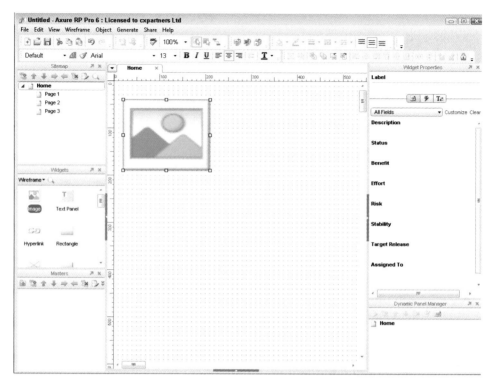

FIGURE 6-94: To add an image, first drag an image placeholder from the Widgets pane onto the canvas.

Axure will ask you if you want to auto size the image. Auto size means it will import the image in its original size. You have already sized and positioned your image object; you want the imported image to match it.

❺ Click No.

If you are importing a large image, Axure will ask if you want to optimize it. This is a good idea because it reduces the file size and image quality isn't that important for your wireframe.

❻ Click Yes.

Your image will replace the image placeholder (see Figure 6-95). You can now reposition or resize it.

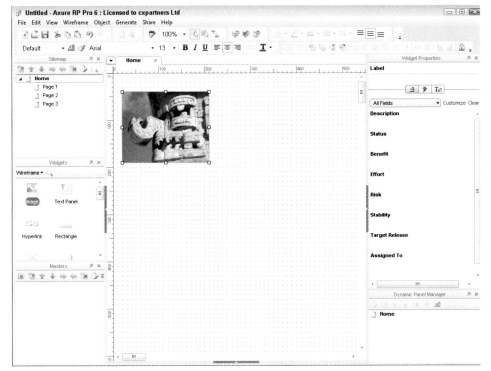

FIGURE 6-95: Once you choose your image, it will replace the image placeholder.

Creating custom buttons

It's tempting to use the default buttons from the Axure widget library, but they can make your wireframe look a bit ugly. The problem is that when you export the prototype, the default buttons display as default operating system buttons. Here's how to create custom buttons:

❶ Drag a Rectangle onto your canvas from the widgets pane.

❷ Right-click the Rectangle, choose Edit Button Shape, and then choose Rounded Rectangle.

❸ Adjust the corner radius by clicking and dragging the small yellow triangle on the top-left corner of the shape (see Figure 6-96).

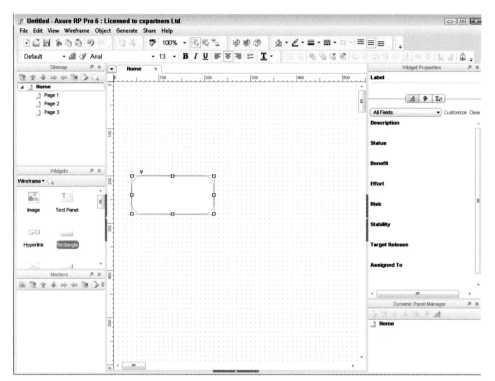

FIGURE 6-96: Dragging the small yellow triangle above the top left of the rectangle adjusts the corner radius.

tip Editing the button shape is really useful for creating various interface elements. For example, the Rounded rectangle top option gives you the perfect tab shape.

To shade the button, follow these steps:

❶ Open the Fill Color drop-down.

❷ Change the fill type from Solid to Linear Gradient. A strip of color will appear that defaults to a white to black gradient.

❸ To change the color of the gradient, select a color slider and then choose a new color from the palette. For this exercise, change the white to a light-ish gray.

❹ Do the same with the black color slider and change it to a darker gray.

❺ You can change the position of the colors in your gradient simply by dragging them left or right. Move your darker gray slider about a quarter of the way in from the right.

6 Add another color to your gradient by clicking just below the gradient strip at the point you want to add your color.

7 Change this third color slider to a lighter gray and move it to the far right (see Figure 6-97).

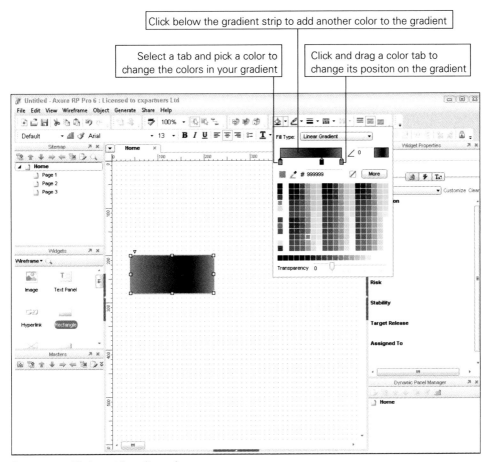

FIGURE 6-97: Working with gradient colors.

8 To make the gradient run from the top of your button to bottom, you need to change the angle. Use the angle adjuster and set it to 90 degrees.

9 To finish the button, add a thin dark gray outline and white text to make it stand out against everything else on your wireframe (see Figure 6-98).

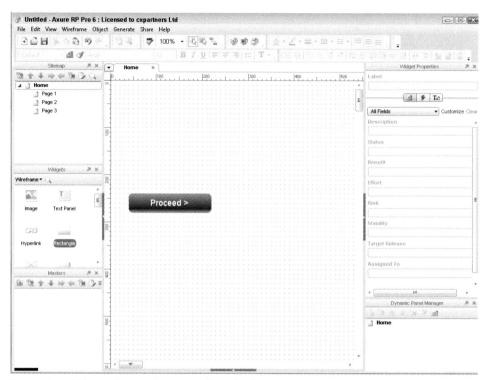

FIGURE 6-98: Adding gradients to shapes gives them affordance.

Creating master objects

Axure has a really useful feature called a master object. It allows you to save elements you have created as masters that can be used elsewhere on your wireframe. Anything you turn into a master object will appear in the master objects pane. That makes it easy to re-use them as you can drag them onto any page.

The best thing about a master object is that if you edit it, every instance of that object within your wireframes is updated. This means it's perfect for headers, footers, or widgets that need to be the same on all pages.

To create a master object:

❶ Select all the objects you want to include in your master.

tip Make sure every element that you want to include in the master object is selected before right-clicking them.

② Right-click your selected items, choose Convert, and then choose Convert To Master (see Figure 6-99).

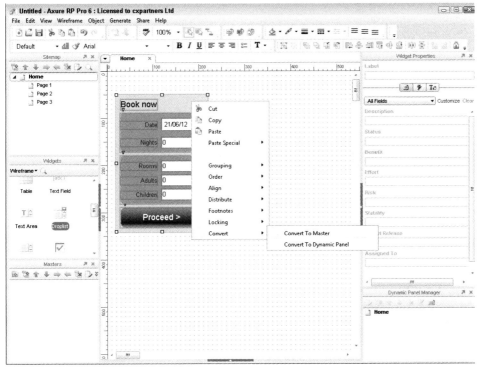

FIGURE 6-99: Converting to a master.

③ A popup displays, asking that you name your new master object.

All your objects should be grouped and highlighted in red. Your object will also appear in your Masters panel and will have the name you gave it in Step 3 (see Figure 6-100).

④ You can now add multiples of your master object by dragging your new object from the Masters pane onto your canvas (see Figure 6-101).

⑤ To edit a master object, simply double-click it either in the Masters pane or on any instance of it on your wireframe. Save your changes and then all instances of your master object will update (see Figure 6-102).

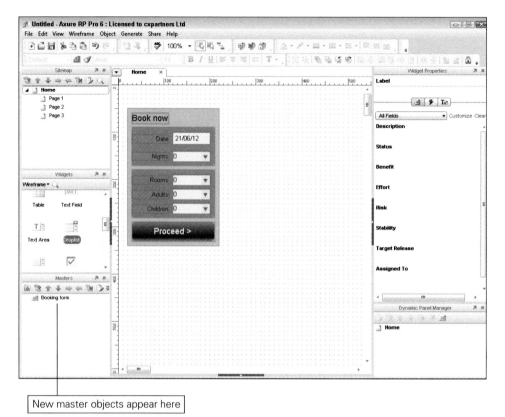

New master objects appear here

FIGURE 6-100: Your new master will appear in the Masters pane.

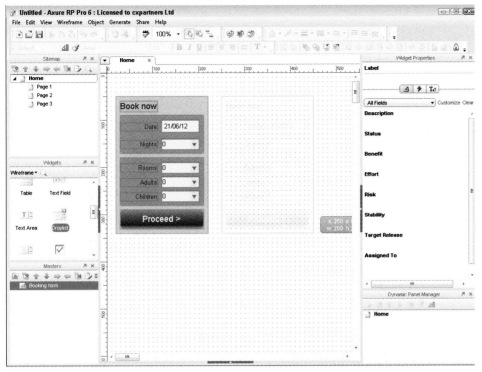

FIGURE 6-101: You can drag as many copies of your master object onto the canvas as you want.

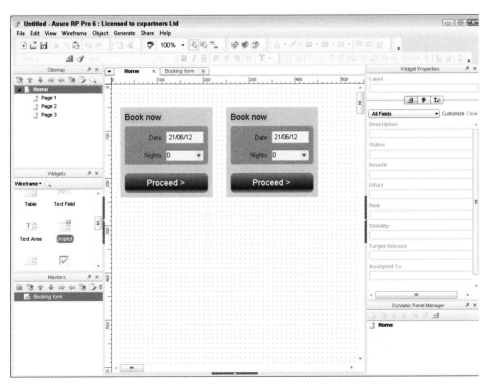

FIGURE 6-102: When you edit a master object, all instances of that object will be updated.

HOW TO Create wireframes in PowerPoint

PowerPoint is often overlooked as a wireframing tool. However most (if not all) of you will know how to use it on at least a basic level and will have it or Keynote installed on your computer making it very easy for teams to share the files.

If you are a Keynote user, there are differences in the drawing tools, but the same basic guidelines can be used.

PowerPoint's drawing and layout controls are a bit more crude than Axure's or OmniGraffle's controls. Still, it's fairly simple to get up to speed with PowerPoint and you can communicate exactly the same level of information that you can in either of the other packages.

Setting up the template

This section shows you how to set up the template so it's easier to create wireframes in PowerPoint.

Enabling Snap to grid

Make sure that snap to grid is turned on before you do anything. It will help with the positioning of elements and allow you to align everything more easily.

To turn on snap to grid:

1. Right-click the slide background and select Grid and Guides. You can also change the spacing of the Grid in this display.

> **tip** Once a shape is selected, by default the cursor controls will move the shape one grid space. To move it one pixel at a time, hold down the Ctrl key (hold down the Alt key on a Mac) and then use the cursors.

2. Snapping objects to other objects or snapping to shape can get annoying for wireframing; we recommend that you turn it off and that you also turn off smart guides. See Figure 103.

FIGURE 6-103: The Grid and Guides dialog with the Snap objects to grid selected for wireframing.

Adjusting sizing

Sizing for screen resolution presentations (1024 px by 768 px, for instance) isn't as accurate as in OmniGraffle or Axure where you can work in actual size.

A neat trick is to paste a screenshot of a site with the page width and type the size that you're after. Scale it down to fit on the page and then use the font size tool in PowerPoint to match this size.

Body copy can look small (6 pt or 7 pt) but still be readable.

One option is to set the page layout size to A2 landscape (59.4 cm by 42 cm). This allows you to create your wireframes in actual size.

Either way, you'll find yourself frequently magnifying in and out of slides.

To set the slide size:

❶ Go to the Design tab and click Page Setup. The Page Setup dialog box displays.

❷ Enter custom sizes in the Width box and Height box (see Figure 6-104).

FIGURE 6-104: Customizing sizes in the Page Setup dialog.

Creating wireframes

With your template set up, you can begin to add the elements needed to create wireframes.

Creating the page outline

The page outline for the example wireframe is simply a rectangle with a mid-gray outline (see Figure 6-105). Depending on what you are wireframing, you'll probably need to keep bringing it forward so it sits in front of the other elements.

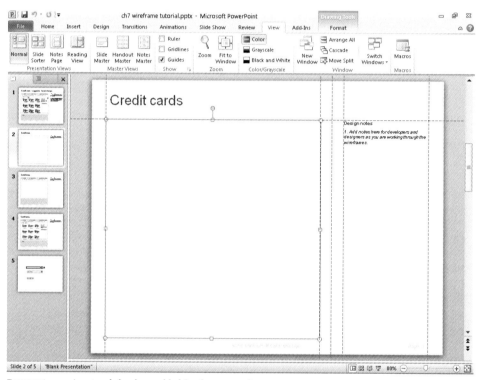

FIGURE 6-105: A rectangle has been added for the page outline.

Creating the tabbed navigation

The ordering of objects on top of each other is how you create several of the visual effects (for example, tabs).

1. Place three rectangles within the rectangle to form the header, body, and footer areas of the page. Shade the header and footer in a slightly darker gray to the body.

2. Add the text for the navigation.

❸ Select a rounded rectangle from the Shapes menu and make it the same color as the page body. This ensures the two areas visually link together—and then place it so that it strides the content and navigation areas.

❹ Any text that you have already placed on the slide will need to be brought to the front. The tab can then be placed beneath the relevant navigation link (see Figure 6-106).

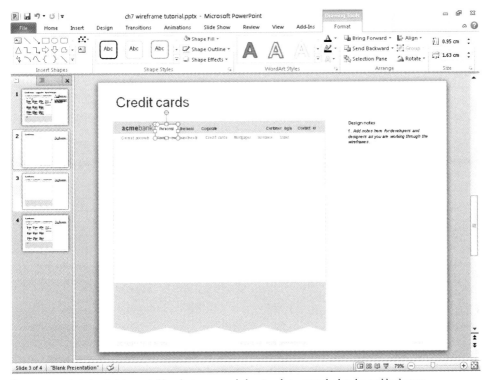

FIGURE 6-106: A simple tab created by placing a rounded rectangle to span the header and body area.

Styling shapes

There are only five elements you control when styling shapes. In PowerPoint, you are constantly playing with these five things:

> **The type of shape used.** Rectangles are most common, but you will also use rounded rectangles and triangles.

tip PowerPoint has a Change Shape command (see Figure 6-107) in case another shape works better (it retains any styling you might have already applied).

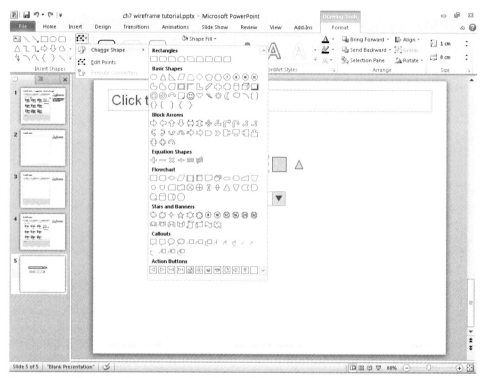

FIGURE 6-107: The Change Shape command provides a useful way of switching the selected shape while retaining its styling.

> **The color of the fill.** Typically, this is just a matter of playing with shades of gray to see how it affects the visual heat of the elements on the page and how they work together. For some shapes, such as buttons, you might apply a gradient to suggest affordance. If you click the Shape Fill button, select Gradient, and then select More Gradients, it displays a detailed control panel where you can control the colors and position of the gradient within the shape.

The Fill option within the Format Shape window (see Figure 6-108) gives good control over the appearance of the fill and allows you to add gradients

FIGURE 6-108: Changing the appearance of the fill and adding gradients.

> **The color of the outline (if used).** Outlines are generally reserved for form elements.

> **The size of the type.** The type size depends on the hierarchy of the element on the page. For example, is it a heading or is it body copy?

> **The color of the type.** Depending on the shade of gray used, you can control the visual emphasis given to any piece of text.

Combining shapes

Elements such as drop-downs are created by combining different shapes.

To create a drop-down:

1 Place a rectangle, a square, and a triangle on the canvas.

2 Remove the outline from the triangle and rotate it 180 degrees. Shade it dark gray.

3 Shade the square to a mid-gray and place the triangle in the center of it, resizing where necessary.

4 Shade the rectangle with a pale gray and type the text you want to display.

5 Group the shapes, so that they act as a single element that can be moved around the page—the text in the drop-down field will still be editable. See Figure 6-109.

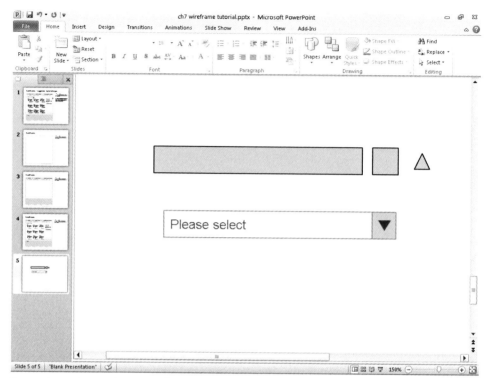

FIGURE 6-109: A rectangle, square and triangle have been joined together to create a simple drop-down menu.

Usability Test Reports

7

USABILITY TEST REPORTS ENABLE YOU TO communicate the findings of a usability test to the project team. You might be doing this as part of the project team (involved directly in its development and release) or as an external contributor. Either way, it's a critical time in the project lifecycle. The outcome of the testing will affect the future development and release of the product or service.

In this chapter you will learn what makes a good usability test report (see Figure 7-1), what you need to communicate, the types of audiences, note-taking tips, and research ideas.

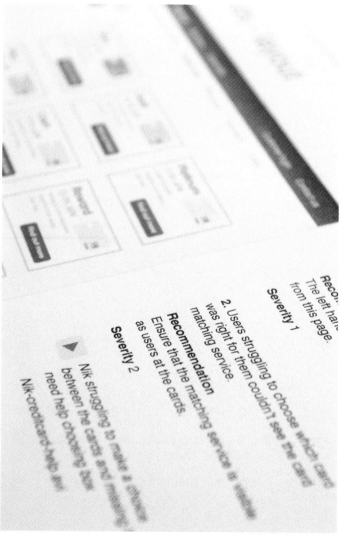

FIGURE 7-1: A usability test report showing an interface, the problems uncovered, and suggestions for improvements.

What makes a good test report?

A usability test report clearly communicates what was uncovered in the user research. A great report enables the project team to discuss actionable solutions that improve the product or service for the users.

When to create a test report

Developing a clear report on how the service is used will help to gain the trust that everything is working as it should or create the necessary buy-in for changes that need to be made. The level of detail and style of report required can vary depending on:

> **The test objectives.** This is what you've been asked to uncover.

> **The audience.** Understand that different roles in an organization want to hear different things.

> **The project stage.** For example:

- Use benchmark testing at the beginning of a project to understand the current situation and what the competition is doing. You uncover the paths to follow and the pitfalls to avoid.

- Use validation testing on wireframes or pre-launch designs to generate amends to feed back into the projects development.

- Use standalone testing to understand and improve an existing product or service.

> **The desired outputs from the testing.** What's going to happen with the findings? Will they be prioritized as part of a phased rollout? Or will they be implemented immediately as part of an agile or iterative process?

> **The time you have to turn it around.** This will affect the depth of your report.

What are you communicating?

Test reports can often be verbose Word documents on all the issues uncovered, occasionally with a screenshot to illustrate the problem. These reports usually gather dust on desks and are difficult to make sense out of.

Instead a report should be actionable by the project team and show at minimum:

> What is working well and what users like (usability testing isn't just about the problems).

> What isn't working and needs to be fixed.

> How to fix the problems.

This last point is crucial and often omitted, but the purpose of a usability test or expert review is to make a meaningful difference in the design of the product or service. Actionable recommendations will make that difference.

Anatomy of the perfect test report

A user test report (see Figure 7-2) should give clear context to the research findings. It should show the team what was uncovered and spark discussion around the improvements that need to be made.

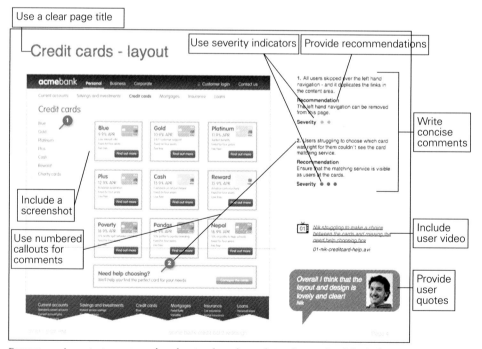

FIGURE 7-2: A user test report template showing the web page being discussed and the findings from the research.

Use a clear page title

Base each page on a single topic (for example, navigation) or a theme (for example, a user-experience theme such as trust). Make the title as straightforward and succinct as possible.

Include a screenshot

Show the project team the exact screen being referred to and where the problems occurred. The numbered callouts shown on Figure 7-2 refer to numbered comments listed on the right of the document.

Write concise comments

Comments should neatly summarize the problem found or observation made. Make sure you stick to one comment per item number.

Provide recommendations

Include suggestions to overcome problems. Unless you know the site well, frame these as discussion starters and involve the project team in developing the final recommendations.

Use severity indicators

Severity indicators are placed below each comment and are a good way to help the project team understand the extent of the problems. These can be used in conjunction with commercial factors (such as the cost to implement the change and the expected uplift in sales from it) to help prioritize changes. In Figure 7-2, severity is simplified to a four-point score and indicated by the colored dots:

- Three red dots: All users had problems

- Two amber dots: Some users had problems

- One yellow dot: A minor problem

- Green: A comment or observation

Provide user quotes

User quotes help provide reality to the presentation. Use a quote or two to summarize how users found the page—good or bad.

Include user video

Including videos that illustrate the experiences and frustrations users have is a brilliant way to persuade teams that change is needed.

Additional slides to include in your test report

These are examples of other templates that are frequently used to help build the final presentation. Figures 7-3 through 7-9 walk you through these templates, providing you with a visual representation of the content.

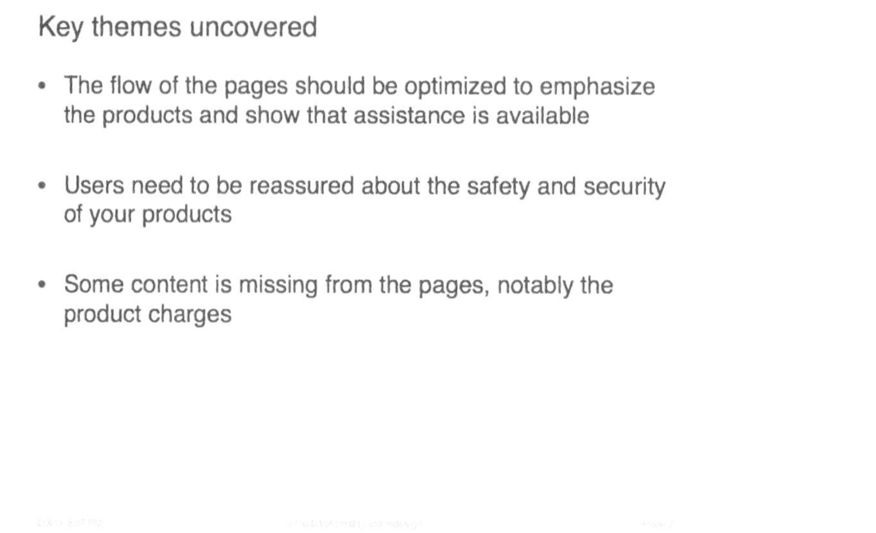

Key themes uncovered
• The flow of the pages should be optimized to emphasize the products and show that assistance is available
• Users need to be reassured about the safety and security of your products
• Some content is missing from the pages, notably the product charges

FIGURE 7-3: Key themes uncovered is a simple template pulling out the key themes that you found and are presenting. It gives focus to the rest of your presentation.

Who we interviewed
Nik, 32
Young professional
Loved the clarity of the site
Name, Age
Segment
Key thought
Previous experience

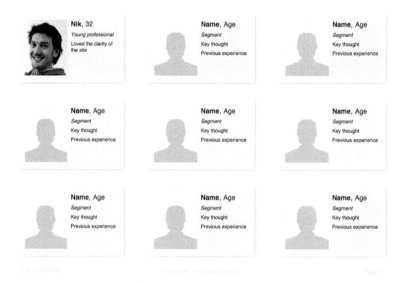

FIGURE 7-4: Who was interviewed focuses on the users with whom you tested. You can enhance the profiles by including logos of the brands with which they had previous experience.

FIGURE 7-5: A simplified layout that is good for presentations with project overseers.

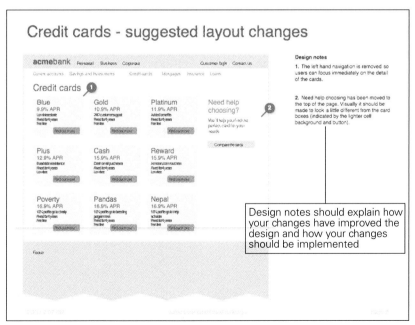

FIGURE 7-6: A suggested layout changes slide is helpful for the frequent occasions when you reach the end of a test and have ideas for how the changes should be implemented. You can draw these up as sketches or wireframes and give examples of where others have successfully solved the problem.

note Design notes should explain how your changes have improved the design and how your changes should be implemented

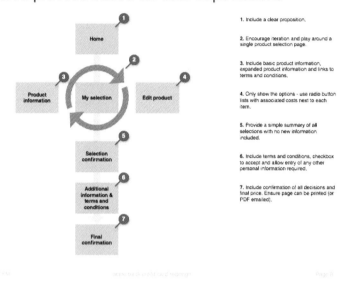

FIGURE 7-7:A Revised process based on user expectations slide is helpful when user tests and expert reviews uncover fundamental problems with the user journey through a product.

tip Understanding user expectations for how the process should work and remapping the user journey creates significant differences in the site's success—things will then work the way a user expects them to.

note You might also include simple text outputs or examples using colorblindness checks to help illustrate accessibility issues.

Recommended code changes

```
<form>
  <fieldset><legend>Personal information</legend>
    <label for="name">Name</label><input type="text" id="name" />
    <label for="email">Email</label><input type="text" id="email" />
    <label for="dob">Date of birth</label><input type="text" id="dob" />
  </fieldset>
</form>
```

1. Ensure that label tags are included.

2. Use for and id tags to link the label to the associated input.

Note: A new feature of HTML5 is the ability to add default placeholder text. Within the input tag include:

```
placeholder="default value"
```

FIGURE 7-8: Recommended code changes—yep, really. Snippets of HTML are often included to illustrate how an element of the page should be recoded to make it more usable or accessible.

Key findings table

Description of problem	Issue type	Severity	Design effort	Dev effort	Cost	Page #
All users skipped over the left hand navigation - and it duplicates the links in the content area.	Navigation	1				p4
Users struggling to choose which card was right for them couldn't see the card matching service.	Page flow	2				p4
Users need the fee to be qualified.	Content	2				p5
Users had questions about the safety and security of the credit cards that aren't answered on this page. This would stop several users from applying.	Content	3				p5

FIGURE 7-9: A Key findings table provides you with a prioritization of recommendations.

> **note** Prioritization is best achieved through collaboration with the project team, and can help assess effort and cost required against the potential gains from making a change. Later in this chapter, you'll learn some workshop ideas to assist with this.

Who is the audience?

Understanding the audience will help to shape your approach to reporting the findings. Here are some of the character types we meet and work with on a regular basis:

Those who roll their sleeves up

The people who roll up their sleeves are often the project managers, designers, and developers. They want to get involved with the testing and the findings. Most importantly, they want to help shape the recommendations and be keen to make them a reality.

Those who just want the findings

Design teams and internal UX teams often just want to understand the findings. It may be that they didn't have the internal resources to run the testing themselves—which they might be perfectly capable of doing. They have strong ideas on all aspects of the testing, so it's worth involving the early sharing proposed plans, document formats and drafts. They understand their products better than you do and are capable of developing their own design solutions.

Those who trust your expertise

The project team trusts your expertise and wants the best product possible. They want to understand your recommendations in order to implement them and care about the impact of the changes in terms of time and cost. They will help you liaise with the right teams to get the changes implemented.

Those who want the big picture

These are often the marketing directors, business owners, and senior managers. They want to be able to take a step back and see how users are interacting with their products and services to see where improvements must be made. They're also interested in the broader user experience—what the users are up to offline, where else they are looking and who they are talking to.

Note-taking and research tips

In order to put together a good report, it's important that you have clear notes that you can use as a starting point.

After the testing, these notes can be analyzed and sorted to help uncover the emerging themes.

Because user tests are conducted at different points in the design process they have different objectives. This can affect the type of report you produce and therefore the notes that you take. The following sections discuss a number of methods to account for the different report needs.

Taking notes for exploratory tests

In-depth exploratory tests are carried out at the start of the design process or for a comprehensive website review (benchmark testing or standalone testing, for instance). They require a comprehensive report and you need to record a broad range of findings, including:

> What's working well.

> Usability issues that need fixing.

> Missing information or functionality that users need to complete their task.

> Where the site fails to match the users' mental model.

> Interesting user behaviors.

> User quotes to back up usability issues or recommendations that you make.

So you need to capture a lot of information, which leaves you with a large amount of text. Picking out the really useful bits can be difficult. Here are some useful techniques for creating more manageable notes.

> Start a new set of notes for each participant (it doesn't matter if it's on paper, in Excel, or in Notepad).

> Divide notes up into web pages visited. Whenever a user visits a new page write that page as a title then note what happens below it.

> Time stamp your notes. Marking a time next to your notes will make it easier to find a specific point when you go back over them. If you take the time from the computer being used for testing it will help you easily find video clips to back up specific points in your report.

Coding your notes

Use a code system (see Figure 7-10) to help you find specific pieces of information. This simply means assigning a symbol to each type of information you note down, for example:

> " (Quote mark)—Something interesting a participant said.

> ! (Exclamation mark)—An error occurred.

> * (Star)—A note that relates to a key testing objective.

> ? (Question mark)—Participant was confused.

> + (Plus)—A positive point.

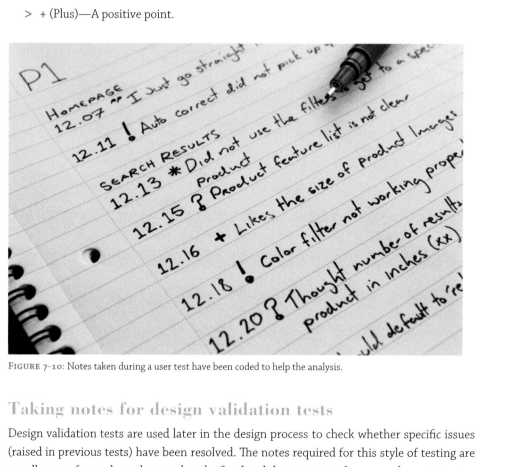

FIGURE 7-10: Notes taken during a user test have been coded to help the analysis.

Taking notes for design validation tests

Design validation tests are used later in the design process to check whether specific issues (raised in previous tests) have been resolved. The notes required for this style of testing are usually more focused on what needs to be fixed and the output is often amendments to wireframes or designs.

A simple technique for taking notes is to print out the designs you are testing (see Figure 7-11). Make notes on the appropriate pages as the participants work their way through them. A good idea is to use a different color pen for each participant. This makes it really clear which issue was found by whom and how many different participants found the same issue. Focus your notes on what needs to be changed or tweaked, and you end up with an easy-to-work-through list of amendments.

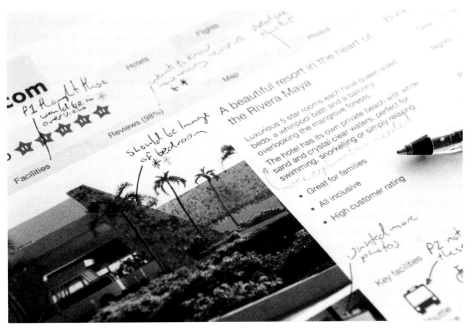

FIGURE 7-11: Notes from user testing have been made directly onto print-outs of the screens.

RESEARCH AND WORKSHOP IDEAS

Once your user testing is complete, you will have a ton of issues to report. Simply listing every issue one by one, in the order you found them, can make the report seem disjointed and hard to read. The report needs structure.

Facilitating workshops helps structure the final report and, more importantly, encourages discussion (and ownership) of the findings with the project team.

WORKSHOP IDEA: Identify themes

The best way to get a structure for a report is to base it on themes that are common across the various issues you found (we've included a few examples in the list that follows). A simple and effective way to spot themes in your findings is to write all the issues down on Post-It Notes and stick them up on a wall. Group Post-Its with similar issues together and your themes will start to emerge.

Here are some ways you could group your issues:

> **User-experience themes** (such as trust issues, learnability, and user expectations)

> **Task/goal-based themes** (tasks such as finding products, making payments, and finding information)

> **Severity-based** (group issues according to how severe a problem they are for users)

> **Page functionality** (specific areas like search, navigation, or calls to action)

We frequently run this workshop with the client soon after the testing (sleeping on the findings can help balance the discussions). We encourage clients to make their own notes and sticking them on a wall. At the end of the sessions, we start to cluster the notes into the themes.

note Refer to Figure 1-7 in Chapter 1 for a visual example of clustering.

This process gives clients ownership of the findings and helps to make them meaningful for their organization or the project that they are working on.

WORKSHOP IDEA: Prioritize findings

Prioritizing your findings and recommendations is a useful way of giving the product managers, designers, and developers a clear set of guidelines for taking their website forward. The order in which you prioritize your findings should take into account all aspects of designing and developing a website, not just the user requirements. It's best to involve all the relevant stakeholders in a prioritization workshop to determine the final order.

Your prioritization of issues should take into account:

> **Severity** of usability issues.

> **Impact** that any changes will have on the business. Will solving the issue be worth it? Will it generate more money? Could it potentially lose money? Just because resolving a usability issue may have a positive impact on the user experience, it may have a negative impact on the business.

note We worked on a project for a ticketing website in 2010 where one of the recommendations we considered was to skip a step in the booking process. This, however, would have meant a big loss in ad impressions from the page we wanted to skip and ultimately a loss in revenue for the business.

> **Feasibility** of the project. How much development and design effort will it take to fix the problem? Can the proposed recommendations be achieved with the business's current capabilities?

Conducting a prioritization workshop

To workshop the final prioritization, create a table that has a column for all the issues in the report and a column for severity ratings. Include a column for page reference numbers so people in the workshop know where to look to find more detail on the issue. Include extra columns for impact and feasibility ratings. These will be filled out during the workshop.

Go through the list of findings and, as a group, assign a rating to both feasibility and impact for each issue. It helps to transfer the issues onto Post-It Notes and use color-coded stickers (see Figure 7-12); this makes the workshop more visual and collaborative for the attendees. The issues with the highest combined score have the highest priority.

> **note** While these examples use "impact on the business" and "feasibility" as factors in determining prioritization, it's important to know that the factors you use may be different for your business or client depending on your goals.

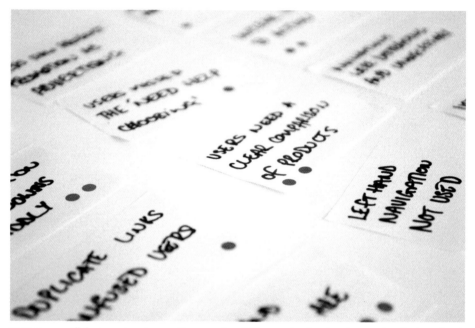

FIGURE 7-12: All the issues have been written onto Post-It Notes and ratings have been assigned using colored stickers.

WORKSHOP IDEA: Practice presenting the findings

Once you have completed the report you could simply hand it over to the design and development team and wave goodbye to it. But if you really want to get across how important the issues in the report are, and convince the stakeholders that they really need to make updates, you need to give a presentation.

Practicing your presentation (see Figure 7-13) is essential to making sure it all goes right on the big day. When you do a practice run, don't just sit at your computer and go through it in your head. Stand up and speak aloud, run it though a projector, and get somebody to sit and listen.

FIGURE 7-13: Practicing the presentation with your peers helps you to work through the best way to express the findings clearly.

Reading through the report aloud will give you an idea of how long it will take. If your report is going to go on longer than time allows, think about what the most important points you want to get across are and focus on those.

Getting someone to sit and listen is always worthwhile. He can tell you if what you're trying to get across is being communicated properly and where to improve.

Running the presentation through a projector will show you if the audience can see the report clearly. Slides that look good on your screen will not necessarily show up well when projected across a room.

If you need them, check that you have speakers—and triple check that any video you use works.

What are the simplest ways to communicate the findings?

When project schedules are tight you don't always have time to craft a beautiful report. Sometimes you need to get the issues you discovered across as quickly and simply as possible. Here are some ways to do it.

Use structured email

It sounds obvious but a well-structured email based on the key themes from your testing can be enough to get your message across. Use bold text to indicate the themes and list the findings below each theme. It's always worth sending an email of the key themes anyway so everyone knows what to expect from the report.

Spreadsheets can be used in a similar way, but the formatting of them can get too fiddly.

Use annotated screenshots

If your notes were written on printouts of the designs tested, then sharing those directly with the designers can be more useful than a full-blown report. It shows them exactly where all the issues are and what needs fixing.

The projector method

One simple technique that can be used at several points in the design process is to project what you are testing onto a whiteboard. Then simply annotate directly onto the whiteboard and take photos to send to the project team.

Share post-testing workshop photos

If you went through the process of identifying these or prioritizing findings, sharing photos of those groups is quick and easy. It is a good way to get across an overview of the testing in a short period of time. Better yet, involve the project team in the workshop.

HOW TO Create a report in PowerPoint

Sometimes you will need to create a formal presentation of your findings. To be effective, the information you are communicating needs to be clear and persuasive.

Creating a robust document structure will help you to put together reports more efficiently. And, if they are well designed, they will ensure that audience or reader can understand the problems users had and the improvements that need to be made.

> **note** You can download the example files from http://cxpartners.com/resources, but there are some helpful tips and tricks in this section to help you create and modify your own documents.

Other chapters focused just on the creation of the specific elements; this chapter also covers some PowerPoint basics.

Setting up the template

This section provides a quick introduction to setting up master slides, which will help you to break free from the default templates shipped with PowerPoint. It can take your presentations from being the same as everyone else's to being beautifully crafted and memorable.

Editing the slide master

To edit the Slide Master, follow these steps:

❶ Create a new presentation.

❷ Go to View, choose Master views, and then choose Slide Master (see Figure 7-14).

Any changes you make in this view will affect all the slides in your presentation (except the title slide). The text boxes can be moved, fonts changed (color, size, type), and elements such as company logos added to appear on all slides. See Figure 7-15.

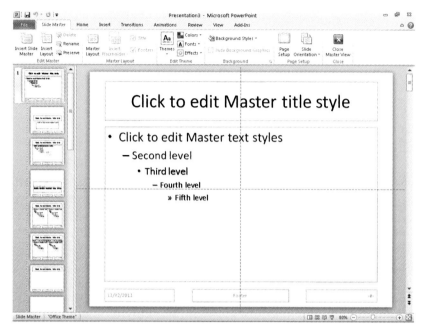

FIGURE 7-14: Before any changes are made to the Slide Master.

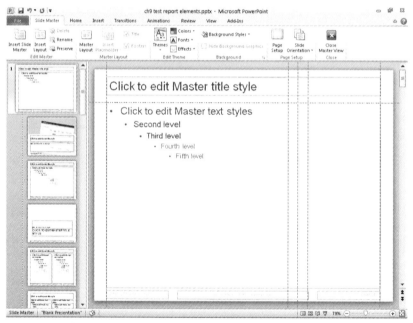

FIGURE 7-15: After some changes have been made to the Slide Master.

Between Figure 7-14 and Figure 7-15, the main elements were aligned to the guides that are being used throughout the example presentation. The bullets have been made to a uniform style and the color changed to the magenta that's used elsewhere in the presentation. To revise bullets:

① Select the text box and go to the Home tab.

② Click the Bullets drop-down arrow and choose Bullets and Numbering.

③ In the Bullets and Numbering dialog box that displays, you can customize the shape and color of bullets used.

Editing the Title Master

Once you are in the Slide Master View you can easily access the Title Master from the left panel (see Figure 7-16).

note In PowerPoint versions before 2010, the Title Master may have to be added as an extra step.

The elements on this page can be moved around and styled in the same way as on the Slide Master.

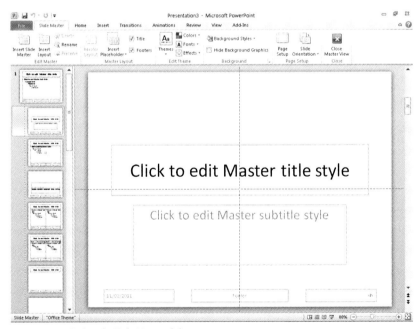

FIGURE 7-16: Before the Title Master slide revision.

Figure 7-17 shows the following revisions to the Title Master slide:

> Text is styled by changing the font, making it smaller and coloring it gray.

> Title and subtitle are aligned to the guides.

> An image that expresses the content of the presentation is added and arranged it so it appears behind everything else.

> A plain white box is given 25% transparency so that the text stands out on top while the image can still be seen behind.

> A text box for names and date is added.

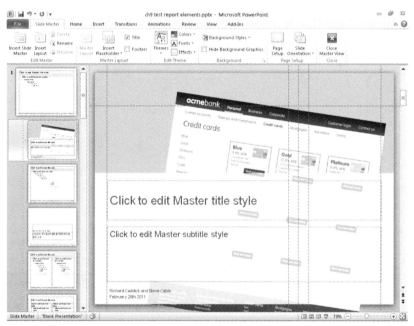

FIGURE 7-17: Revising the Title Master slide.

Once you have finished editing the Slide Master, go to the Slide Master tab and click the Close Master View button.

Creating a custom color palette

To create a custom color palette:

❶ Click the Design tab.

❷ In the Themes group, click the Colors down arrow, which displays the list of default color palettes available.

❸ At the bottom of is list, click Create New Theme Colors, which displays the dialog box shown in Figure 7-18.

❹ In the Create New Theme Colors dialog box, update the default colors used for all elements.

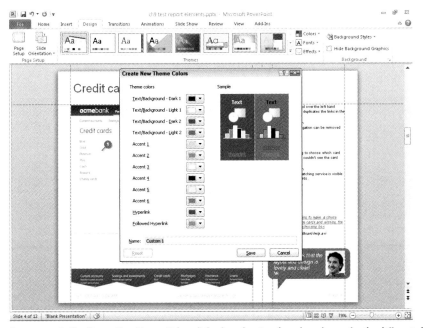

FIGURE 7-18: The Create New Theme Colors dialog box showing the colors chosen for the different elements.

It takes a little experimentation to get exactly what you're after. There are some surprise restrictions, such as not being able to remove the outline surrounding objects.

Using guides

Guides help you to keep items in the same place on each page of your report. You can use them to help position the screen being referred to, the notes, callouts and user quotes. Figure 7-19 shows where we've put the guides in our template and how we've aligned objects to them.

> To turn guides on and off, go to the View tab and select the Guides checkbox.

> To move a guide, click on the guide and drag it.

> To add a new guide, hold down Ctrl (Alt on a Mac) and drag the guide.

> To remove a guide, drag it off the presentation canvas.

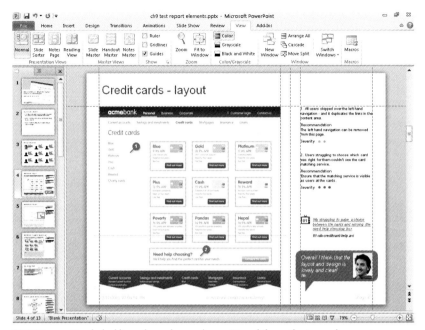

FIGURE 7-19: The dashed lines show where we've positioned the guides in our document.

Creating the report

The following tips will help you create effective styles for your PowerPoint documents.

Editing text boxes

Learning how to change the default behavior of text boxes will enable you to better control the styling of your presentations.

Setting margins

The default margins on text boxes can get in the way of the alignment you are trying to achieve. To get around this, right-click the text box (or other shape with text in it) and select the Format Shape controls. Click the Text Box tab and set all Internal margin settings to 0. See Figure 7-20.

Paragraph controls

To neatly lay out the text, you need to get into the line spacing and paragraph spacing controls. Generally you'd use a single spacing line height with increased spacing before each paragraph.

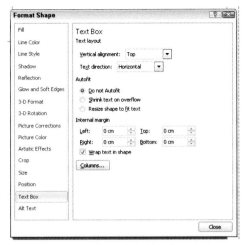

FIGURE 7-20: The Text Box dialog box showing the Internal margins set to 0.

❶ With the text box selected, click the Home tab.

❷ In the Paragraph group, click the spacing icon.

❸ Choose Line Spacing Options at the bottom of the menu.

❹ In the Paragraph dialog box that displays (see Figure 7-21), adjust the spacing before the paragraph.

FIGURE 7-21: The Paragraph alignment dialog box with the spacing before the paragraph set to 5.4 pt.

Editing images

Here are some useful editing tips to use once you've inserted an image.

Crop

With the image selected, use the Picture Tools formatting palette to select the Crop tool (see Figure 7-22). Once you've cropped an image by dragging it inward, you can un-crop it by using the same tool and dragging outward.

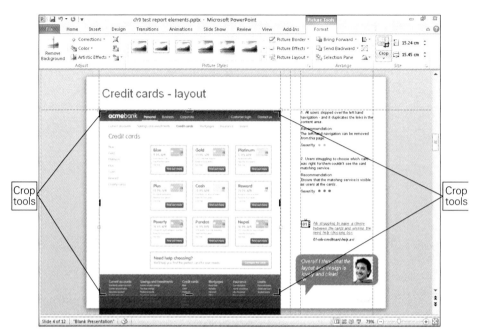

FIGURE 7-22: Using the Crop tools.

Transparency

Image transparency (on JPGs, GIFs, PNGs, BMPs, and so on) isn't available on a PC. To solve this problem, you can place a white box over the image and give it a transparency of 25%. To set transparency, follow these steps:

❶ Right-click the shape and click Fill.

❷ Click the Solid Fill option.

❸ In the Fill Color box, click and drag the Transparency slider to 25% (see Figure 7-23).

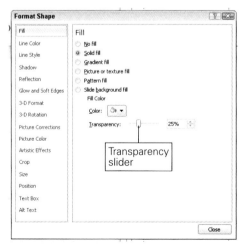

FIGURE 7-23: A semi-transparent white rectangle is placed in front of an image to make the image appear to have transparency.

On a Mac, add a transparency by double-clicking the image and adjusting the transparency in the Fill tab.

Creating custom elements

Some of the default shapes in PowerPoint are a little crude and both hard to control and style. You can, however, create some custom elements that are easy to make and simpler to style.

User quote callouts

A *user quote callout* is simply a rounded rectangle grouped with a right triangle.

Draw the rounded rectangle first and use the handles to adjust the corner radius—this isn't possible with the standard callout. Remove the outlines and turn off shadows.

Draw the triangle and rotate it 180 degrees using the formatting palette. Again, remove outlines and turn off shadows.

Place a text box on top of the rounded rectangle. For this example, move the right edge of the text box toward the left to allow space for the user photo to be inserted. See Figure 7-24.

FIGURE 7-24: Creating a user quote callout.

Note indicators

Note indicators are created by grouping a circle with a 45-degree line. The number is put directly into the circle (without using an additional text box) and text is centered both horizontally and vertically.

On the Home tab, use the Shape Fill and Shape Outline tools to choose a color for the note indicator that contrasts well with the site you are testing. Use the Shape Effects tool to add a shadow to help lift the note indicator from the page. See Figure 7-25.

FIGURE 7-25: Creating a simple note indicator.

Inserting video

The simplest way to link to a video is to create a hyperlink to it from a text reference on screen:

1 Right-click the text and choose Hyperlink.

2 Browse your computer to find the file you want to link to, select it, and then click OK.

When the presentation is viewed in Slide Show mode, the hyperlink is active.

tip Perhaps a better approach when giving presentations is to embed the video into the PowerPoint. Simply go to the Insert tab, click on Video, and then browse to your file.

When you give the presentation, make sure that you have speakers for the audio.

tip We've found that linking to and embedding videos from PowerPoint isn't without it's problems. So here's an easy way to find the right video in the middle of a presentation if the technology doesn't behave. Create a simple referencing system for each of your video clips. Number them in a single folder in the order that you want them played. Then use that number within video reference in the PowerPoint slide. For example, video01, video02, and so on.

chapter 8

Funnel Diagrams

FUNNEL DIAGRAMS ARE used in web design, development, and management to show how many users pass through a certain route on a website. They show the number of users who travel through a set of pages (for example, a checkout process) as well as how many users complete the process, how many users drop out of the process, and where the dropouts happen. The data for these diagrams are from funnel reports generated by analytics packages and are used to monitor the performance of certain areas of a website.

This chapter is about taking the data from those reports and presenting it in an easy-to-understand diagram that helps provide a compelling argument for updates to a website. See Figure 8-1.

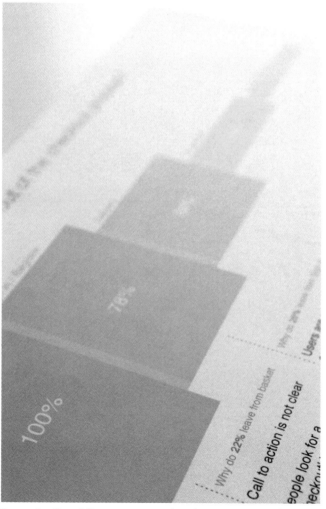

FIGURE 8-1: Funnel diagrams present analytic data in an easy to understand way.

What makes a good funnel diagram?

The funnel diagrams in this chapter are about taking a complex set of data, usually read by analytics experts, and presenting it in a way that is easily understandable by a wider audience. They show how many users visited each page in a process in order to examine which points are causing users to leave. Presenting this data in the right way to the right people at the right time can help put into action changes that are needed to improve the performance of a site.

When to create a funnel diagram

Checking the conversion figures in your analytics package should be a regular exercise. The funnel diagrams in this chapter are used at key points in website development when a clear visualization of data is required to convey to the project team where users are dropping out of a website and why.

When you need to convince stakeholders that there is a problem

Funnel diagrams are a great way to visualize issues with routes through a website. They clearly show where the issues are on a website and also *why* the issues are occurring. They encourage the team to start thinking about possible solutions.

When you must convince stakeholders that a problem needs to be fixed, a funnel diagram like the one shown in Figure 8-2 can get the message across clearly and concisely.

FIGURE 8-2: Funnel diagrams are a good tool for persuading stakeholders that areas of the website need fixing.

When you need to conduct user testing

Funnel diagrams and user testing reports sit together closely and help inform each other.

Funnel reports that are generated by analytic packages are a good way to inform and structure a user test such as a checkout or booking form. A funnel report can show you where most of the users are leaving the website, which tells you where the problem areas are. This lets you know what areas of the website need investigation during the user testing sessions.

Once the testing is complete you can use your findings to feed into the final funnel diagram. If your test was structured around the pages that were causing users to leave the website, then you should uncover some of the reasons why users are leaving. These reasons should be included in your funnel diagram to show why users might be leaving the website at each step in the process. For example, users going through a checkout process might get to the sign-in/register page and not want to create an account, so they decide to shop elsewhere.

It's good to include a funnel diagram in a testing report whenever it is appropriate. For example, if the test was performed on a checkout or a form, a funnel diagram shows an overview of the whole report. It summarizes every page in the process that was tested and the key findings for each page.

Testing is often sparked by low conversion rates (for example, when the percentage of users who complete the checkout is lower than the number of users who added items to their baskets). Showing the results of user testing against a funnel diagram based on conversion rates will clearly show an answer to the business' key question: Why is this happening?

What are you communicating?

A funnel diagram is designed to show two things: *what* users are doing along a key journey through a website and *why* they are doing it. The way you present this data can have a great effect on the way the reader interprets it. This section explains what you need to include in your funnel diagram and how to represent the data in a clear and compelling way.

The *what* and *why*

The *what* comes from web analytics tools that measure the number visitors who visit specific pages on a website. Better known examples are Google analytics, Omniture, and Webtrends. Analytics tools also generate funnel reports that show conversion rates through a user journey. These show how many users pass through a set sequence of pages, like a checkout process. At each page in the process it shows how many users continued onto the next page and how many left the website. This is important because it shows you where most users are leaving the process so you know where improvements to the site can be made.

Funnel reports show the exact number of users who visit each page. It also displays the percentage of users who visit each page based on the number of users who started the process. However, the funnel reports generated by analytics packages are not always the easiest to read. Understanding the important information can be difficult for those who aren't familiar with using analytics tools (see Figure 8-3).

For example, if 100 users start a checkout process by putting items in a shopping cart, then the number of those who click the Buy button and move onto the next page in the checkout will be represented as a percentage of the initial 100 users. This percentage usually decreases at each page in the checkout process. What you end up with is a view of how many users started the checkout, and what percentage of them actually finished and paid.

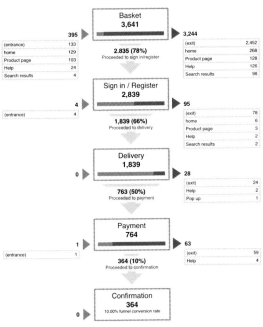

FIGURE 8-3: A typical funnel report looks something like this.

The *why* comes from user testing, in-depth interviews, call center listening, or any other form of user research. You need to communicate findings from user research that help explain why users might be leaving the website at certain points in the process. It might be key findings from user testing or common questions that the call center receives. Adding insights about why users are leaving pages in a process, next to the relevant points in a funnel diagram, creates a compelling user-centered view of the performance of a website.

Fundamentally what you are trying to communicate is what pages in a process are causing problems and why they are causing problems. You need to communicate the information from these two sources in an easy-to-understand way. Doing so creates a single page that shows a convincing argument that the current process is not working for your users and needs to be fixed.

The project team can then collaborate on ideas that help to resolve the issues.

Representing the data

Funnel diagrams are based on funnel reports, but the display of the data should not be shown as a literal funnel. That's because the funnel metaphor requires lines similar to those plotted along a graph causing the drop out to be displayed as a gradient moving from a tall shape to a shorter shape. In Figure 8-4, it looks as though users were leaving the basket page gradually as the graph moves toward the sign-in page—one by one over a period of time.

| 100% | 78% | 52% | 21% | 10% |

| Basket | Sign in / Register | Delivery | Payment | Confirmation |

FIGURE 8-4: The diagonal lines make it look like there is a gradual decrease in visitors between pages.

This is a misrepresentation of the data because you can't tell from analytics that users left the page one by one over a period of time. You know only that a certain number of users visited the basket and a certain number of users visited the sign-in page. All you can accurately show is how many users landed on each page. A much clearer way of illustrating this is to show each page in the process as a separate block (see Figure 8-5). The height of each block represents the volume of users who visited that page, and you can clearly see the reduction in users between each step.

FIGURE 8-5: By using decreasing the size of each block, you can more accurately represent the number of visitors on each page.

Using percentages

The data that you get from analytics show how many users pass through a set of pages and this data can be represented in a number of ways. The three examples shown in Figure 8-6 show the same data represented three ways:

> **Example A** shows the actual number of users on each page. This gives an accurate representation of the data, but requires the reader to work out the percentage differences between each page. Percentages are also more useful for tracking the performance of a funnel over time. Seeing that 10% of users completed the checkout process in Month 1 compared to 15% in Month 2 shows a clear improvement in conversion.

> **Example B** shows relative percentages—the percentage of users who moved onto the next step based on the number of users on the previous page. The example shows that 66% of users who were on the Sign In page moved on to the Delivery page. It illustrates the performance of individual pages, but does not give a clear view of overall performance and it is not easy to see exactly how many users finished the process. The data set shows the last figure as 47%, which works out as 10% of the users who began the process by entering the Basket page. It is common for this data to be misinterpreted so the drop out does not seem so bad—the drop between the Payment and Confirmation pages could be misinterpreted as 3%, when in fact its 47%.

> **Example C** shows overall percentage and is the recommended method. Each percentage shown is based on the number of visitors who started the process. It's easier to see from this sequence that there is a steady decline in visitors across the pages. You can

clearly see that only 10% of users who started the process actually finished it. The information tells the story in an easy-to-understand way.

	Basket	Sign in	Delivery	Payment	Confirmation
A.	3,641	2,839	1,893	764	364
B.	100%	78%	66%	50%	47%
C.	100%	78%	52%	21%	10%

FIGURE 8-6: The data from funnel reports can be represented in three ways.

Anatomy of a funnel diagram

Figure 8-7 shows a breakdown of what you need to include in your funnel diagram and how to present it.

Use a title that explains the purpose of the document
A title like "Why do 90% of users drop out of the checkout?" describes the goal being studied and clearly makes it a user-centered rather than a data-centered document.

Use blocks to show the number of users who visited each page
Using blocks to represent the percentage of users who visited a page helps to show at a glance where the big drops in visitors are. Make sure the difference in size between each block is an accurate representation of the dropout figures.

Keep all the widths equal to show that each page has equal importance in the process.

Base the percentages on the number of users who started the process
It's clearer to see drops in visitors when reading overall percentages of visitors on each page. It also shows how many visitors overall managed to finished the process.

Use shading to emphasize visitor numbers

For greater visual impact, fade out the key color at each step as the number of visitor decreases. Be careful not to fade it out so much that the text in the blocks becomes unreadable.

Use text size to emphasize visitor numbers

Decreasing the text size depending on visitor numbers helps to show which pages are doing well and which are not doing so well. Start with the smallest number (10% in this case) making sure that it is at a readable size, then make the text in each block bigger as the numbers increase.

Include the key issues with each page

Write two or three key issues for each page that you found during user research. Place these issues under a heading for that page and visually it link it to the appropriate block. This shows why pages might be performing poorly.

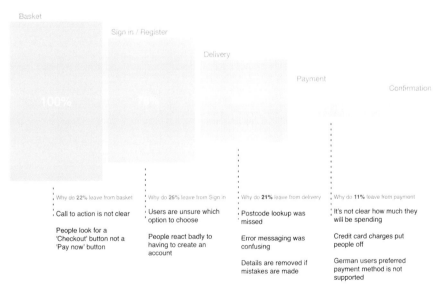

Why do 90% of people drop out of the checkout process?

FIGURE 8-7: A completed funnel diagram that shows how many users completed the process as well as any usability issues that might be causing users to drop out.

Who is the audience?

Funnel diagrams are similar to user testing reports in the way that they are used to explain the performance of a site from a user perspective. They often form part of a user test report and are aimed at a similar audience. This audience is made up of two groups.

The development team

Members of the development team are the people who will be coming up with the solutions to the problems shown in the funnel diagram. The reasons for the drop in the number of visitors on each page are important because it gives them the insight they need to collaborate on solutions.

The product managers and senior stakeholders

Product managers and senior stakeholders want to know how well their product is doing at the moment as well as how they can improve it. For these people it's all about convincing them that changes need to be made. The numbers are going to be the most important thing for them to see. The big drops in visitors will be the most convincing argument that they need to fund a project and fix the problems. Alternatively, it can confirm that a project they have already initiated is the right thing to do—therefore their funding is well spent.

In previous projects, for example, you've seen how the money spent on user experience has been paid back through increased revenues within a few weeks of the project going live.

RESEARCH AND WORKSHOP IDEAS

The data for your funnel diagram comes from two main sources:

> Analytics tools to understand *what* pages might be performing poorly

> User research to learn *why* users might be leaving a website before finishing a process.

RESEARCH TECHNIQUE: Get to the *what*

The *what* comes from analytics tools. The default funnel reports they create give you all the data you need to explain what is happening in the process. You need to do is decide which set of pages or what process you should use for your funnel report.

Focus on the key user journeys of your site. What is it that users come to your site to do most often? What are the key goals they are trying to achieve? This might be a specific journey like a checkout process or a set of forms. It might also be slightly more open, such as searching and browsing for products and adding them to the basket. Previous user journey documents or task models might well determine the pages you evaluate for the funnel diagram.

Look for the unique journeys that users are taking through a process. Your pages might be step 1, step 2, step 3, but you'll frequently see that user journeys bounce between the pages. This is particularly true where a key piece of information isn't displayed clearly. For example, use your analytics tool to generate funnel reports for unique journeys, such as:

step 1, step 2, step 1, step 2, step 3

or

step 1, step 2, step 3, step 2, step 3

In addition to the key goals of the users, you need to consider the goals of the business. Check the performance of journeys that relate to specific strategic aims or key performance indicators. (KPIs). For example, if your goal was to steer more customers toward certain sets of products, did you succeed?

RESEARCH TECHNIQUE: Get to the *why*

The *why* comes from user research. Look for insight into why specific pages in the journey are stopping users from completing their visits. These insights can be found in the forms of user research covered here.

User testing

Get users to think out loud as they try to complete the tasks and talk to them about anything they find difficult or confusing. Your goal is to understand any problems they encounter. The number of users you talk to in user testing is often low, but it enables you to get a better understanding of why problems might be occurring and what state of mind users might be in when trying to complete the journey. See Figure 8-8.

FIGURE 8-8: User testing the pages within your funnel report can help you understand the problems that cause users to leave the process.

Call-center listening

Listen in on calls through to the customer service department of the business, and interview the call-center staff. You want to know the the most common complaints they receive about the pages within your funnel report and the questions that aren't being answered online which prompts the call. Call centers often keep a record of the types of calls received, which can provide some useful insights. See Figure 8-9.

FIGURE 8-9: Listening in on calls from users can uncover common issues with the website.

Website feedback tools

Tools like Opinion Lab (www.opinionlab.com/) enable users to leave feedback on specific areas of the website. If the business already has tools like this in place then it is always worth getting information from them. This has the potential to get you a high volume of feedback. What it does not always tell you is why the user had an issue, and how badly it affected their journey.

It's important to remember that the more research you do, the better your data will be. It's a good idea to mix your research methods in order to get a spread of both:

> **Quantitative data** (high numbers of comparable data). For example, from analytics, website feedback tools, and surveys.

> **Qualitative data** (lower numbers of detailed information). For example, user testing and call-center listening.

Website feedback and call-center listening are a good start to get an idea of what issues there might be; user testing allows you to investigate those issues in more detail.

HOW TO Create a funnel diagram in OmniGraffle

In this section, you'll learn how to create a funnel diagram in OmniGraffle, including how to create all the necessary shapes and text elements.

Setting up the template

To set up the canvas for a funnel diagram, follow these steps:

1. Go to File and click New to create a new document.

2. Go to File, choose Page Setup, and then change the paper size to A4 so the diagram will scale well when printed.

3. Change the orientation to Landscape so the diagram will fit into a presentation slide.

4. Open the inspector and in the Canvas section, click the Size option.

5. Set the Ruler Units to pixels (px).

6. In the Canvas section, click the Grid option.

7. Set the Major Grid Spacing option to 100 px and the Minor Grid Steps to 10.

8. Make sure Snap to grid is selected. See Figure 8-10.

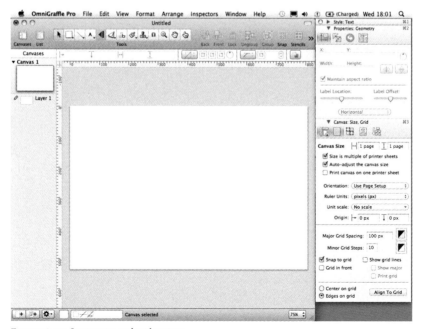

FIGURE 8-10: Setting size and grid options.

Creating the diagram

In this section, you'll learn how to represent the pages in the funnel and how to represent the amount of users who visited each page. You'll also learn how to present the usability issues associated with each page.

Representing the pages and percentages

❶ Select the Rectangle shape tool in the toolbar and draw a rectangle for each step in the process.

Figure 8-11 shows five rectangles that represent the five pages in the checkout process.

❷ Go to the Style part of the Inspector and deselect the Stroke checkbox in Lines and Shapes; repeat this for the Shadow checkbox.

❸ Make sure each rectangle is the same width as the others, so they all have equal emphasis.

> **tip** The rectangles need to all fit with space on either side of the page. Five rectangles each 150 pixels wide fit comfortably.

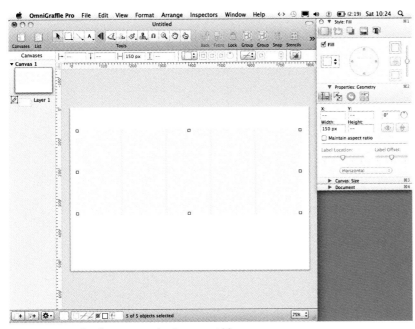

FIGURE 8-11: Make all your rectangles the same width.

④ Type the percentages for each page into each corresponding rectangle (see Figure 8-12).

⑤ Make each rectangle the same number of pixels high as its respective percentage. For example, the 52% block should be 52 pixels high (as shown in Figure 8-12).

note To set a shape at a specific height use the geometry controls in the properties part of the Inspector.

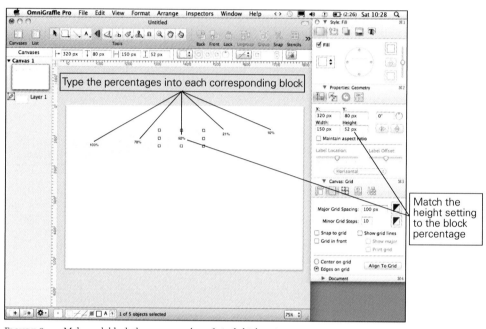

FIGURE 8-12: Make each block the same number of pixels high as its respective percentage.

⑥ Align all the rectangles along their horizontal centers using the alignment options in the Canvas section of the Inspector (see Figure 8-13).

⑦ Group all the rectangles using the Group button at the top of the canvas (or use keyboard shortcut Shift+Cmd+G).

⑧ Resize the group vertically to around 250 pixels high.

They will now fit on the page, but the ratios between the rectangles will be an accurate representation of the percentages written on them. See Figure 8-13.

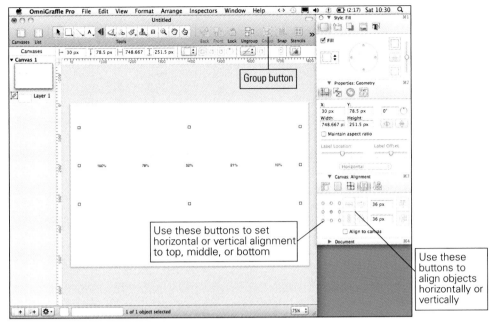

FIGURE 8-13: When you resize your rectangles as a group, the ratios between stay the same.

9 Open the Style part of the inspector and within the text options click the Font button (it looks like a capital A). This opens the Font panel.

10 Adjust the text size of each of the percentages to emphasize the numbers. (For the lowest percentage, choose a size that is small yet still readable.)

We've used 12-point text in our example. As you move back through the steps, increase the font size by two points for each step. The font sizes in the example are 20-point, 18-point, 16-point, 14-point, and 12-point.

11 Use the style part of the Inspector to change the color of the text on each block to white.

12 Add color to the rectangles to emphasize drops in numbers using the style part of the inspector. (Choose a color for the lowest percentage that is light, but still able to show up the text.) Make each rectangle darker as you move back through the steps. See Figure 8-14.

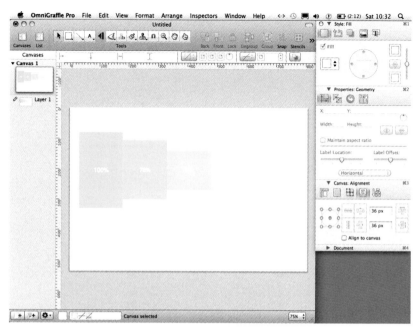

FIGURE 8-14: Use color and text size to emphasize the numbers written in each rectangle.

⓭ Draw another rectangle, color it white, and set the opacity to 20%. Make it 10 pixels wide.

⓮ Duplicate the rectangle and put one over the right edge of all the colored rectangles (except the first rectangle).

⓯ Make the opaque rectangles the same height as the colored rectangle they're sitting on (see Figure 8-15). This helps visually separate each block.

⓰ Select the Text tool from the Toolbar, add a text box above each block, and then type the relevant page name. This makes it clear which page each rectangle represents.

⓱ Using the text part of the style panel in the Inspector, change the font size to 12 point and the font color to a 60% gray. As shown in Figure 8-16, this makes it clear enough to read but does not put too much emphasis on it.

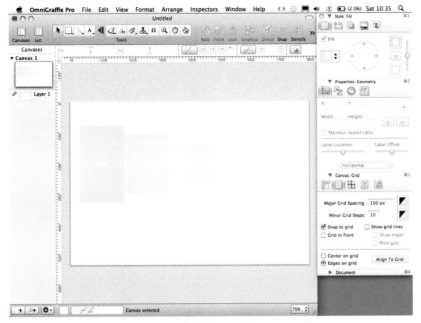

FIGURE 8-15: Adding thin, opaque rectangles helps visually separate each step.

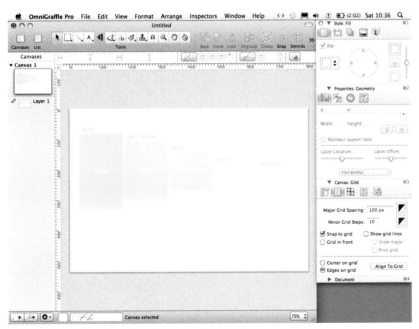

FIGURE 8-16: Titles make it clear what page each rectangle represents.

Adding the *why*

To add the usability issues for each page:

❶ Select the Text tool from the Toolbar and create a text box that is the same width as one of the rectangles (in this case, 150 pixels).

❷ Place it under the first box and type Why do 22% leave the basket.

> **note**   The page name and the percentage you write in your header should reflect the name of the page the issues are on and the number of users who left this page without continuing through the process.

❸ Use the text options in the style section of the Inspector to change the font size to 9 point and the font color to a 50% gray (see Figure 8-17).

FIGURE 8-17: Make the text box the same width as one of the rectangles that represents a page in the funnel.

❹ Type the key issues for this page below the header. (Include only one or two key issues per page; otherwise the document can become cluttered.)

> **note**   Leave at least a one-line gap between each issue to make it easy to identify individual points.

5 Make the font size of the issues 11 point and the font color 25% gray (see Figure 8-18).

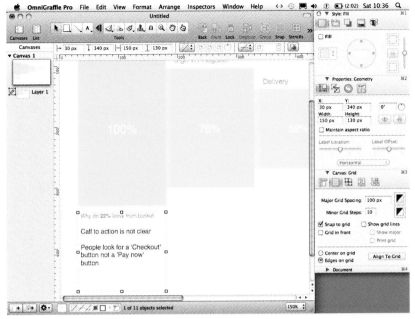

FIGURE 8-18: The issues should be in a font that is slightly larger and darker because this information is the most important.

6 Copy and paste the text box so you have one for each of the pages.

7 Align them all along their top edge using the alignment controls in the canvas section of the Inspector.

8 Once you have all your issues written and aligned, place each text box so it sits directly below the page it corresponds to.

9 Select all the text boxes and move them right so they sit between the block they correspond to and the next block in the process (see Figure 8-19).

10 Click the Line tool from the Toolbar and draw a line vertically from about 10 pixels below the center of the first block down to the text box. Draw the line past the heading in the text box below and stop at the first issue typed in the box.

11 Repeat this for all the rectangles and text boxes. This visually links each text box with the page it corresponds to.

12 Once your lines are drawn, select them all.

13 Using the style panel in the Inspector, set the line thickness to 0.5, the line color to a 60% gray, and the line style to a dotted line (see Figure 8-20).

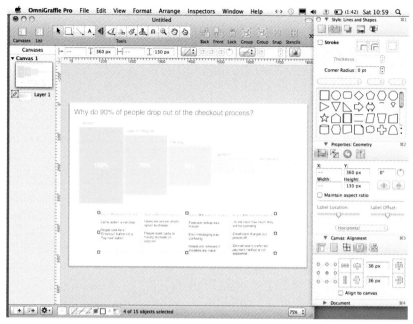

FIGURE 8-19: Each Key issue block should straddle two steps in the funnel.

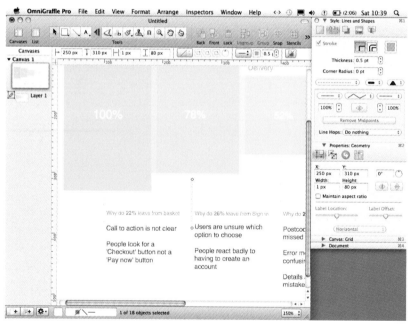

FIGURE 8-20: Thin, gray dotted lines visually link each set of issues to the corresponding page without adding too much clutter.

⑭ Finally, add a title (see Figure 8-21). Use a 24-point font and use a dark gray color.

note Make sure your title explains the purpose of the document. For example, "Why do 90% of people drop out of the checkout?"

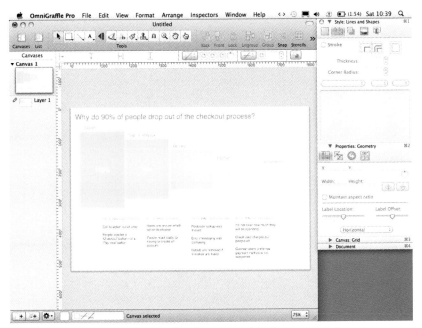

FIGURE 8-21: A descriptive title can explain the purpose of the document and also make a strong statement about how many users dropped out of the process.

HOW TO Create a funnel diagram in PowerPoint

In this section, you'll learn how to create a funnel diagram in PowerPoint, including how to set up the page and create all the elements necessary for the diagram.

Setting up the template

This funnel diagram will be designed in a landscape layout, which is usually PowerPoint's default layout. If you do need to change the page orientation, you will find it in the Design tab under the Slide orientation drop-down.

1 Delete the default text panels to clear off the canvas.

2 Change the grid by right-clicking anywhere on the canvas and selecting Grid and Guides.

3 Set the grid spacing to 0.5 and make sure both Snap objects to grid and Snap objects to other objects are checked.

Creating the diagram

In this section, you'll learn how to represent the pages in the funnel and the amount of users who visited each page. You'll also learn how to present the usability issues associated with each page.

Representing pages and percentages

1 Draw a rectangle to represent each step in the process.

Figure 8-22 shows five rectangles that represent the five pages in the checkout process.

2 On the Home tab, in the Drawing group, click the Shape outline drop-down and then remove the outline from the shapes.

3 Make all of the rectangles the same width so they have equal emphasis.

> **note** The rectangles need to fit with space either side of the page. To set the widths of all the rectangles accurately, select them all and use the width controls within the Format tab. As shown in Figure 8-22, five rectangles at 4.8 cm wide will fit comfortably.

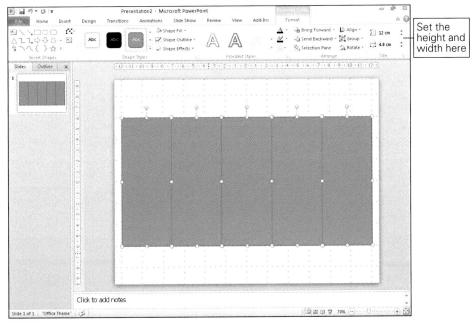

FIGURE 8-22: Make all the rectangles the same width.

❹ Type the percentages of visitors on each page into each corresponding rectangle.

❺ Make the heights of each rectangle represent the percentage in them by using the percentage figures as points in centimeters (see Figure 8-23). For example, 100% is 10.0 cm and 78% is 7.8 cm.

❻ Select all the rectangles.

❼ Align the rectangles to their middles by clicking the Align drop-down in Arrange group on the Format tab.

❽ Adjust the text size of each of the percentages to emphasize the numbers. (For the lowest percentage, choose a size that is small yet still readable.)

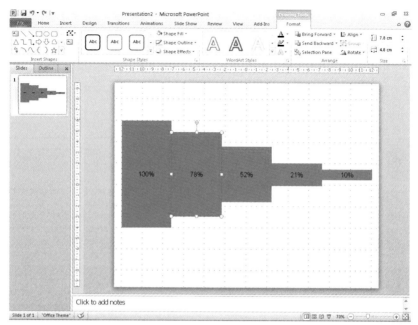

FIGURE 8-23: Set the height of each block to represent the percentage of users that visited each page.

In our example, we've used 12-point text. As you move back through the steps, increase the font size by two points for each step. The font sizes in the example are 20-point, 18-point, 16-point, 14-point, and 12-point.

9 On the Home tab, in the Font group, change the font color of all the percentages to white.

10 Select the rectangle.

11 On the Home tab, in the Drawing group, click the Shape Fill drop-down and then change the rectangle color. Choose a color for the smallest block that is light but still has enough contrast against the white text to be readable.

12 Make each rectangle the same color but slightly darker as you move back through the steps (see Figure 8-24).

13 Draw another rectangle, remove the outline, change the fill color to white, and set the transparency to 80%.

14 Using the Size controls on the Format tab, set the width to 0.5 cm.

15 Put the rectangle over the right edge of all the colored rectangles (except the first rectangle).

16 Make the opaque rectangles the same height as the colored rectangle they're sitting on (see Figure 8-25). This helps visually separate each block.

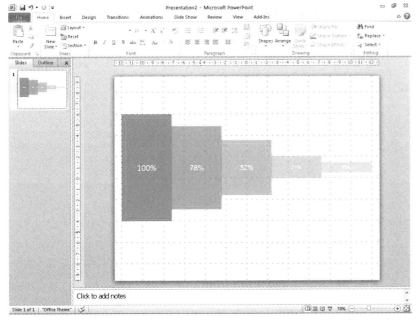

FIGURE 8-24: Use fill colors and font sizes to emphasize the percentages of users who visited each page.

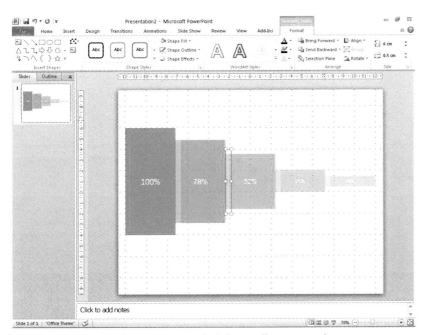

FIGURE 8-25: Adding the thin, opaque rectangles helps visually separate each step.

⓱ Insert a text box above each step and then type the relevant page name into each of them. This makes it clear which page each rectangle represents.

⓲ Using the Font controls on the Home tab, set the font size to 14 point and set the font color to a mid-gray (see Figure 8-26).

note If the flow of the pages consistently fails to meet the users' expectations then it is probable your task model is wrong or needs refining (or you haven't developed one). This will have the biggest impact on the wireframes that you are designing.

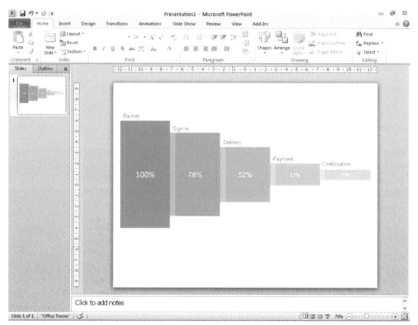

FIGURE 8-26: Titles make it clear what each rectangle represents.

Adding the *why*

To add the usability issues for each page:

❶ Create a text box that is the same width as one of the steps in the funnel (in this case, 4.8 cm).

❷ Place it under the first step and type the header Why do 22% leave the basket.

note The page name and percentage you write should reflect the name of the page the issues are on and the number of users who left this page without continuing on through the checkout process.

❸ Use the Font options in the Home tab to set the font size to 8 point and the font color to a mid-gray (see Figure 8-27).

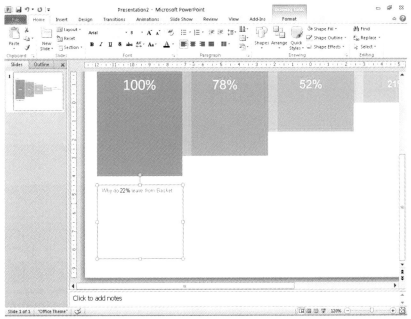

FIGURE 8-27: Make the text box the same width as one of the rectangles that represents a page in the funnel.

❹ Type the key issues for this page below the header (see Figure 8-28). (Include only one or two key issues per page; otherwise the document can become overcrowded.)

tip Leave at least a one-line gap between each issue to make it easy to pick individual issues.

❺ Make the font size of the issues 12 point and the font color a dark gray.

❻ Copy and paste the text box so you have one for each page in the process.

❼ Select all the text boxes and use the Align drop-down on the Format tab to align all the text boxes along their top edges.

❽ Once you have all your titles and issues typed and aligned, place each text box so it sits directly below the page it corresponds to.

❾ Select all the text boxes and move them right so they sit between the block they correspond to and the next block in the process (see Figure 8-29).

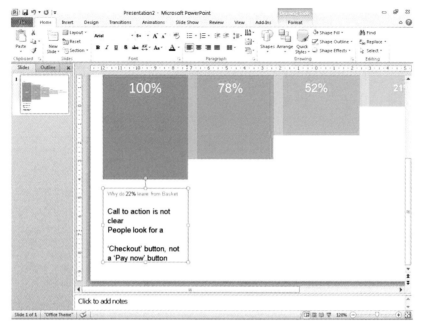

FIGURE 8-28: The issues should be in a font that is slightly larger and larger because this information must be emphasized.

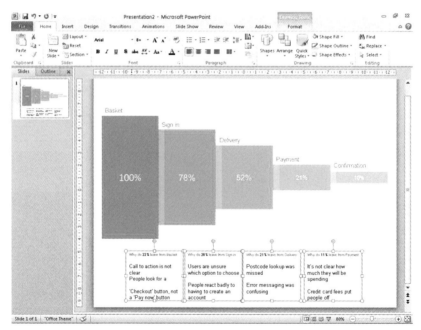

FIGURE 8-29: Each Key issue block should sit between two steps in the funnel.

⑩ On the Home tab, in the Drawing group, click the Shapes drop-down and draw a line vertically starting about 0.5 cm below the center of the first block. Draw the line past the heading in the text box below and stop at the first issue typed in the box.

⑪ Repeat this for all the rectangles and text boxes. This visually links each text box with the page it corresponds to.

⑫ Once your lines are drawn, select them all.

⑬ On the Format tab, in the Drawing group, click the Shape Outline drop-down (see Figure 8-30) to set the line color to a light gray, the weight to 3/4 pt, and the Dashes to Square Dots.

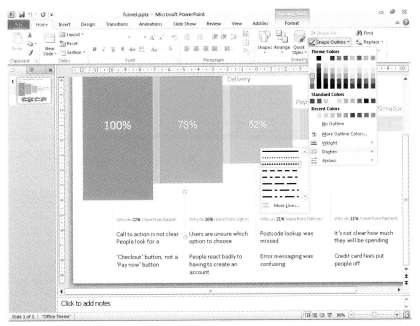

FIGURE 8-30: Thin, gray dotted lines visually link each set of issues to the corresponding page without adding too much clutter.

⑭ Finally, add a title (see Figure 8-31). Use a 24-point font and use a dark gray color.

note Make sure your title explains the purpose of the document. For example, "Why do 90% of people drop out of the checkout?"

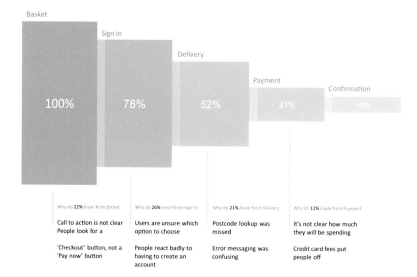

Why do 90% of people drop out of the checkout process?

Basket

Sign in

Delivery

Payment

Confirmation

100%   78%   52%   21%   10%

Why do **22%** leave from Basket

Call to action is not clear People look for a

'Checkout' button, not a 'Pay now' button

Why do **26%** leave from Sign in

Users are unsure which option to choose

People react badly to having to create an account

Why do **21%** leave from Delivery

Postcode lookup was missed

Error messaging was confusing

Why do **11%** leave from Payment

It's not clear how much they will be spending

Credit card fees put people off

FIGURE 8-31: A descriptive title can explain the purpose of the document and also make a strong statement about how many users dropped out of the process.

Index